A Green Fisherman Never Caught A Brown Trout

Essays on Minnesota Ecology

by William Boudreau

Brule Press, Minneapolis

A Green Fisherman Never Caught A Brown Trout

Essays on Minnesota Ecology

Cover Photo by Judy Boudreau. Enhancement by
ProTech, Minneapolis.

Photo credits: pp. 3, 30, 41, 110, and 142 courtesy of
MN Department of Natural Resources; p. 17, Judy
Boudreau; p. 37 Bill Niccum; p. 83 courtesy of the
Lindbergh House; pp. 99 and 113, Gerard Strauss; p.
119, James McCanney; others by the author.

Cover Design: Amy Beyer

"Highway 61 Revisited" originally appeared in *Minnesota Calls*.
"The Ones That Gotaway" was first published in different form in
Stepp'n Out. "Superfish" first appeared in *Sunday Magazine*
(Minneapolis Star-Tribune). "Flyer Fever" in amended form was
initially featured in *Lakeland Boating*. Part of "10,000 Dying
Lakes" was first seen in *Twin Cities Reader*. Portions of other
stories have been published in *Outsport Magazine*.

for Judy

Contents

Chapter 1

Southeast

A Green Fisherman
Never Caught a Brown Trout

There are two kinds of fisherman: The first regards fish as objects for our pleasure, to be exploited as is our wont. After all, are they not cold-blooded, nutritious, delicious (assuming you are too young to have been raised on an every Friday diet of parched fish sticks), and saturated with Omega-3 oils, silver bullet for cancer and heart disease?

The second type of fisherman theorizes that since fish have been around 300-400 million years longer than the GOP, they deserve, well not quite 'equality' but say, consideration. While men and women have pushed aside the forests and spread discount malls to the horizon, fish have gone about the business of raising families of 10,000 or more in each dip and pothole on the planet making only such noise as required by a surface somersault at sunset.

You'd think this quiet service should count for something, but then we've never been good at paying bootblacks, janitors, cops and others we forget about 'til we really need them. And we really need fish.

In fact, we are almost fish ourselves, our bodies being 95% of that element in which they swim. The difference between people and fish many have pointed out, is that with us the slime is on the inside.

But if fishing is anything, it's the pursuit of fancy, an absorption into light and air - a gingerly cosmic step about a world of simple charm, sudden violence, and deep beauty.

For a few moments within hooking distance, every sense is alert and at the ready. But like the Cold War, this military competition seems at times a hopeless impediment to real understanding. Fishing rods - like guns - are no way to deal with a sovereign nation.

Somewhere in your career, slipping off to the wild, you will be more concerned with having an experience than fishing. That moment may never arrive for those concerned, alas, with property taxes, insurance and layoffs.

Perhaps that moment will come when you meet *salmo trutta*, a dark-skinned immigrant from Europe. Salmo, or 'brown' trout, has been the path to awakening for many an angler.

Others of the trout clan do not measure up: rainbows are "dumb" in the words of one scientist, too enamored with the thrill of fast water to respond to its dangers; and a larger proportion of brook trout than any other species are apt to be sword-swallowers.

By contrast, salmo trutta has truly amazing compass. Its sense of smell can detect cigarette smoke on a 2-day beard. The lateral line, or main sensory organ on the side of the fish, picks up distant sounds, like that of a size 13 boot sliding off a stone 300' away. And, owning to a unique double lens, its vision is actually more acute <u>above</u> water than below.

Yet, neutralizing this massive intellect is one crucial fact: the brown trout's brain is approximately 20 times smaller than its stomach. (the human brain, by contrast, is larger than the human stomach, except when hungry).

As you slam the car door, dress and stumble down the bank to river's edge, you only hope he will be there, you don't know for sure. But he's very much aware of you.

3

He's lying only inches away from your boot, making use of an overhung bank to conceal himself so completely, you aren't even aware such a sanctuary exists.

Every scintilla of his smaller brain is telling him to lie motionless. Your greater intelligence is spread out like a clothesline.

Fifteen minutes of you concentrating on nature, and 15 minutes of nature concentrating in a brown trout's tummy, will likely tilt the advantage. Fifteen minutes of reflection should catch something.

The secret is to take that 15 minutes and devote it to a study of the environment. Set aside a quarter hour to celebrate a world where the 'highest' form of life lacks a coat against the elements, has poor eyesight and hearing, runs and climbs trees slowly, and has neither claws nor beak. Once in the woods, we are obviously the most expendable item there.

We are only visitors in the natural realm; we no longer fit in. Our brain gives us a tremendous mechanical advantage, but we lack any decided advantage in raw skills. If we had to return to hunting and gathering, we would eliminate a lot of misconceptions about the hereafter in very short time.

This way, you and he will be fresh for the encounter. If you cast to the water too soon, you will be tired and distracted at the instant of the strike.

You are apt to be stunned at the suddenness and power of the brown trout's attack. Like a billion-dollar rocket immobilized by a leaky plastic pipe, you are short-circuited.

The trout meanwhile, is already launched and is approaching maximum velocity when it hits your nymph. There's only a scant second to react: get under control or he is gone. You are stuck on the pad and he is travelling at the speed of brown, red and black light.

Most mistakes and lost fish occur in this frantic first contact. He realizes you did not come for peaceful purposes and you realize he realizes it.

As the brown trout streaks bank to bank digging toward the bottom to find a root or rock, the fisherman is just coming to his senses. The initial task is to get the trout on the reel. Too much loose line out and you won't be able to set the hook in time.

4

Salmo trutta leaps and twists probing with all his might to find that lapse, that open gate. You gentle him onto the reel letting loose line pull between your fingers. He downshifts into the deepest, thickest current.

Now here's the tricky part: set hard, on too short a line, and you'll snap the tippet or pull the hook out of his mouth; set casually, on too long a line, and the meeting is abruptly adjourned--the sharp hook embedded, not in the trout's mouth, but in his mind and thumping heart.

It will require 15 minutes for both of you to get back to normal. So take a moment by the stream to ripen, a green fisherman never caught a brown trout.

Nymphs Emerge
as Trout Favorite

Because trout fisherman are wedded to the April stream trout opener, and since April has a reputation for finickiness - shifting erratically from sunny 60's to snowy gusts - it's wise to take a moment to iron out a pre-nymphtual agreement.

Nymphs of course, are a logical choice for spring. Not only do they comprise 80-90% of a trout's diet, they can be counted on when various insect hatches are delayed by inclement conditions.

Nymphs are the immature stage of aquatic insects. They may live 2-3 years on the bottom crawling over rocky substrate.

Nymph types can be easily identified and imitated, even by the casual angler. The novice stream fisherman need be concerned with only four types of aquatic nymph: the mayfly, the caddisfly, the stonefly and the midge, or blackfly. Kick over a rock in the stream and you will likely see these four.

The midge will be greenish, about 1/4-1/2" long and curled like a shrimp. The mayfly nymph will be larger with a three-pronged tail. Caddis larvae (they do not have a nymphal stage) are worm-like, up to an inch in length and typically housed in a cocoon of sand, silk and tiny sticks which they weave themselves. The stonefly nymph is the largest of the group and has two tails.

As immature insects, they crawl or swim about their business in the layer of the stream closest to the bottom. Despite turbulence all around, here the water barely moves and the nymph is free to contemplate its coming metamorphosis unless dislodged by actively feeding trout or some other disturbance, say a fisherman's boot.

6

Most nymphs grow to 1-1 1/2" before maturity. When they are ready to emerge as airborne flies, they give up their hold on the stream floor and are swept up in the current. They wriggle free of their larval skin and pop to the surface ready to fly — that is, if they are not eaten as they flee the few final critical inches of stream environment.

Feeding trout of course, often move into riffles and dig out nymphs; you can see the process as their tails touch the surface and brilliant flashes bounce off their bodies and into your eye. But during the mass escape of nymphs - the regulated dispersal of millions called "the hatch" - trout lust exceeds instinctive caution and gives fishermen the advantage.

Suppose you're interested in stream fishing but it's intimidating ever since your buddy put out $100 for a fly-tying kit and wound up with a gob of glue and hair resembling a mouse found in the toaster. Simple, just go to your tackle store and ask for: a) caddis emerger (green); b) gold-ribbed hare's ear nymph; c) Montana nymph; d) zug bug or wooly bugger; and e) midge, in sizes 10, 12, or 14 (approximately $1.85 apiece). Also get line floatant paste, sink coat and tiny split-shot.

If you're using a fly rod, equip yourself with two reels, one floating fly line (riffles) and the other a sinking tip (deep pools); spinning fishermen need an ultra-light outfit with 2-4# test. Pull on a pair of waders or hip-boots and sidle into that cool, clear, highly-oxygenated water.

Nymph imitations are weighted in order to be fished below the surface - often near the bottom - and thus have the added advantage that they can be fished on ultra-light spinning equipment as well as a fly rod. They are particularly well-suited to the smaller streams of southeastern Minnesota.

These are narrow streams so you can cover the best lies from a position in the middle of the stream. Since trout face upstream and have excellent peripheral vision <u>above water</u>, wear 'earth tones' of green and brown and bend close to the stream.

This is short-line fishing where plunking the nymph imitation 15-20' upstream and/or across is all that's necessary. Day-glow orange, yellow, green, etc. lines are easier to follow as the line progresses downstream; strike indicators are very useful leader additions.

Fly line provides an edge because it can be more easily dressed and because the longer rod allows more precise placement. Both spinning and fly fishermen depend on the last few feet of line to deliver the goods and that few feet is mono.

If your plan is generic nymph fishing - anything so long as it takes fish - plan to fish close to the bottom where your nymph will look as if it's been dislodged and tumbling in the current. Determine what depth is needed to reach this point and sink coat that amount of line behind the nymph. Put floatant on the rest of the line you have out so that it's visible on the surface. Put a strike indicator (bright, floating piece of cork or foam) between the two sections of line.

Obviously, if fishing pools are several feet deep, you can forget the floatant since you will need to get down near the bottom where the fish are apt to be. Here's where you use sinking tip line or add the split shot a foot behind the nymph.

If, *eureka*, you spot evidence of a hatch and can identify the nymph form emerging, you won't need to mess with the bottom since fish will be active near the surface. Now you can dress your line to 'hang' the nymph just below the surface where the emergers are twisting in terror.

The trick is to coat the mono leader with floatant - except for the 3-4" directly behind the nymph. You want to use sink coat here.

Remember that although bigger trout inhabit the pools, there are fewer of them and they are more heavily fished. A riffle 4-8" deep will not only hold more fish behind each rock, they are likely to have been passed up by other fishermen.

We counsel an either/or approach, because it's difficult to do justice to both with the same line: sinking tip is useless on riffles and floating line - even with split-shot - simply can't get down fast enough in heavy current to entice the big fellows to strike.

Stand downstream of your intended target and cast or swing the nymph directly upstream on the first pass. Draw in line as the nymph tumbles toward you maintaining a light tension on the line. This is important since you probably won't feel a pick-up on a slack line and, besides, setting the hook would be impossible if you're not within a few seconds of a taut line.

As the line approaches your feet, lift the rod tip to keep the nymph moving and maintain tension. If there is no strike, lower the rod and allow the line to drift downstream. When the line extends fully, lift the rod tip again pulling the nymph toward the surface as if it were about to hatch. This basic retrieve advanced outward a few degrees each cast, can be used to cover the whole stream including undercut banks and underneath deadfalls. To detect upstream strikes, look for any holdup in the drift, or line moving vigorously against the current. Across stream strikes and takes downstream are indicated by a downward pull on line or strike indicator.

In larger pools, use sinking tip flyline or add extra shot to mono and count as the line sinks to the bottom (slack); retrieve and recast. Let the nymph sink to within two counts of the bottom. Now, lift the rod slowly and begin your retrieve. Count to five and twitch the rod tip and quickly strip out several feet of line. Pause and repeat.

Again, the idea is to trick the trout into thinking this nymph is on its way to the surface. Trout are opportunistic feeders and will take nymphs all day long in low-light conditions. Cloudy water some 24 hours after a half-inch rainfall is just right for primetime players.

Hard to Match These Hatcheries

Minnesota operates six cold-water hatcheries stocking nearly seven million trout and salmon in state waters each year. Three of these facilities - Lanesboro, Crystal Springs and Peterson hatcheries - are located southeast to take advantage of that area's several fine springs.

Nearly 10,000 gallons of clean, cold, highly-oxygenated water gushes forth from the underworld each minute, gurgling down spillways and raceways, restoring spawners and anointing eggs in a paean to Minnesota creativity and the diversity of the natural world.

Stocking is necessary because the sheer size of the human population of the state has become a player in the delicate game of checks and balances which umpires the wild realm.

A drive to Lanesboro, the largest of the southeast hatcheries, confirms the fact. Every vestige of the high ground is under cultivation with trees appearing only on precipitously inclined slopes or as shade surrounding the farmstead. The attributes of such policy is visible on the average waistline.

Most of us accept this condition and admit no hankering to destroy the machinery that delivered us from round-the-clock toil to 24-hour shopping. But the rain that splashes down in October, or tumbles to the ground as snow in February, finds not grasses and a thick web of roots, but soil meticulously tilled into tiny clusters of loose solids. From Cologne (MN) to Tulsa (OK), America is following the rain.

In southeast Minnesota, downpours turned into vicious floods for several decades marking the turn of the century, wiping out stream life in a torrent of tepid, dingy water. Conservation practices introduced during the 1930's helped stabilize the deteriorating watershed. Yet local conditions had been affected decisively.

Preferred brook trout habitat - water temperature from 50-60 degrees - shrank as streams staggered and slowed under the weight of unwelcome silt. Trout species from Europe - German browns - were introduced because they could tolerate warmer water (60-70 degrees).

The newer species was reputed to be more wary and harder to catch than the native brookies, but the hatchery-raised fish easily succumbed to crude (for trout) methods as a cane pole and worm because it had little fear of people and could not recognize "natural" diet. Stocking became a kind of joke - like Communist elections - with 99% of the stocked fish disappearing as soon as the tank truck left.

The DNR is under tremendous pressure to maintain a fishery of catchable size. The surest way to do this is simply to stock the streams with 2-yr. old trout (10"). But fisheries pros decry this approach.

"Hatchery fish are not much of an addition to the stream," says Bill Thorne, research biologist and acting area fisheries manager for Lake City. "Hatchery-bred trout behave the opposite of wild fish: they come to the surface to feed as if they were about to receive fish chow and they move toward humans, conditioned to expect food with the arrival of a hatchery worker (trout fry and fingerlings are fed 8 times a day).

"Our studies show that half of stocked rainbows of catchable size, and a quarter of browns are actually caught by anglers, the rest die of natural causes, usually predation by kingfishers and great blue heron."

Recent stocking emphasis has centered on fry, or 1" fish. Not only are hatchery costs much lower because the fish are held for such a short time, but the released fish, should they grow to adulthood (less than 2% do, says Thorne) are more "wild" with a better chance for continued survival.

But hatcheries are a vital link between angler and game and not only because they supply catchable fish. Increasingly, hatchery operations are called upon to take the lead in introducing new species, while maintaining genetic diversity and disease-free populations of existing varieties.

11

At Peterson hatchery for instance, Lee Peterson, hatchery supervisor, has spent years trying to develop three distinct brood lines of each species raised there. Importing eggs from outstate operations, Peterson has built up a reservoir of mating individuals that can be crossed with totally different fish so that any possibility of brother-sister mating is eliminated.

"In-breeding has to be avoided," says Peterson, "because problems - crippled fish, egg failures, mutations, survival problems - develop quickly over just a few generations."

Peterson's task is made the more urgent by the fact that "borrowing" eggs from outstate trout farms increases the chance of importing fatal infections: the Lanesboro hatchery has only recently re-opened after a kidney disease in rainbow trout brood stock forced the DNR to destroy its fish and chlorinate the entire facility.

In order to escape such a fate, Peterson locks up its brood stock and conducts only limited public tours (1:30 p.m. - and please don't embarrass yourself by showing up in waders) in addition to establishing self-contained brood lines.

Peterson has also been charged with creating a proper breeding environment for the Atlantic salmon, the 'delicate delinquent' of state hatchery operations (it took a decade just to develop a breeding population). Unlike rainbows and brown trout, which can be released to large holding ponds where they supplement their diet with insects, Atlantics, says Peterson, must be given adequate room and a vitamin-fortified diet. Otherwise, Peterson relates, "they will attack each other, chewing off fins and creating infections which invade the body cavity causing death."

The re-constituted Lanesboro hatchery and the Crystal Springs operation have been given the responsibility of creating a rainbow trout fishery in southeast. This won't be easy because the rainbow is a notorious vagabond.

Some 25,000 rainbow yearlings (10") from Crystal Springs and 50,000 fingerlings (5" - each species has slightly different growth rates resulting in discrepancies in 'fingerling' sizes) from Lanesboro, are scheduled annually for introduction into southeast streams. To date, the program has been spotty with slight evidence that rainbows are establishing themselves in area streams and growing to decent size.

12

"It's basically a put-n-take fishery for rainbows," relates Thorne. "The yearling fish are creeled fairly quickly; the fingerlings over-winter in the streams and are of a catchable size by spring.

These hatchery rainbows are leaving in a week on a big adventure.

"Rainbows favor fast, deep water and there isn't much of that southeast. We only plant them in a handful of streams and then mainly as a fill-in fishery, to add a little diversity. There are only going to be a few fish over 3/4 of a lb."

Ed Stork, Lanesboro hatchery supervisor, admits that the waters southeast are better suited for brown trout. Lanesboro hopes to plant 25,000 yearling browns and 1 million fingerlings each year to supplement natural reproduction. (Lanesboro contributes 160,000 yearling lake trout to inland lakes in northeast Minnesota as well.)

"Species diversity," claims Mark Ebbers, DNR trout supervisor, instead of aggregate numbers, "is how the hatchery program should be measured." Ebbers points out that thanks to the 400,000 lake trout (Isle Royale strain) raised by the Crystal Springs hatchery, Minnesota has met its quota for Lake Superior stocking entirely with native fish.

Crystal Springs also hosts a pleasant experiment called "splake." The name is a contraction of 'speckled' trout (brook

13

trout) and lake trout; the fish is a product of eggs from the laker and milt from the brookie. About 130,000 splake are raised each year for northeast inland lakes.

According to reports, splake are "fun" to grow, being aggressive, attractive and avid eaters. Like many hybrids, they do not reproduce well. Furthermore, they take artificials and feed aggressively in shallow water during summer.

Fisheries science and hatchery skills aim to fill specific niches: providing catchable fish in areas of high accessibility and demand; restocking trout populations lost to natural actions such as floods and disease or limited by lack of suitable spawning grounds; extending fish stocks into newly reclaimed habitat; and introducing exotic species in locales where sufficient untapped forage assures their survival. But the process is not as linear as some would like to believe.

The DNR buy-out of the Peterson hatchery in 1989 for $3.6 million was supposed to nearly double cold-water capacity and make possible several new programs. When the DNR took possession of the hatchery they discovered volume was less than one-third that claimed before sale. The DNR is litigating to recover nearly $1 million.

The former owner of Peterson hatchery, Jim Cady, is now involved in an extensive cold-water aquaculture venture in reclaimed ore-pits on the Iron Range.

Three Prime Streams
and A Watering Hole

There are 350 miles of trout streams in southeast Minnesota. Located in the "driftless area," i.e., untouched by recent glaciation, southeast waters bubble with clear, cold subsurface fluids percolating through porous rock.

These tributaries thread their way from central highlands to the Mississippi River by way of valleys cut over the course of 450 million years from the floor of an ancient inland sea.

Surrounding bluffs are mounds of dolomite (ocean sediment) up to 250' high. Dolomite, a granular rock high in lime and magnesium carbonate, is light in color and, washed into the streams, gives their waters a characteristic milky appearance.

Rich in carbon, dissolved dolomite forms a base solution which can neutralize acids from rainfall and decaying plants. The resulting flow has a high pH (7.5-9) sufficient to give birth to a rich trove of insect life which spend a portion of their lives living (and being consumed) in the riverbed.

Unfortunately, damaging farming practices have left much of the area denuded and prey to occasional disastrous floods. Fortunately, a good deal of this water has been improved by local volunteers and DNR fisheries workers to the point where brown trout proliferate.

The bends and switchbacks of these streams describe a success story in resource management and a unique turning point in environmental philosophy.

In the two decades from 1970 to 1990, the amount of "good" trout water (150-200 lbs. of fish per acre) in southeast doubled to 230 miles; "fair" water nearly quadrupled to 218.

Watershed management, i.e., habitat protection and development - not increased stocking - achieved spectacular gains in stream productivity ("poor" trout water yields about 30 lbs. per acre).

Management can mean simple education - asking farmers to leave trees near the stream's edge - or purchasing easements, fencing and stream rehabilitation. .

Past agricultural practices led to deforestation, flooding, siltation and loss of prime trout habitat. The trout stream ecosystem depends on cool spring water, numerous riffles where aquatic insects - 90% of the young trout's diet - can propagate, and hiding places.

Easements along stream banks not only allow for public access, they also ensure against encroachment by agriculture. Intensive agriculture destabilizes stream banks by uprooting trees whose roots hold the bank in place. It also robs trout of cover provided by native grasses and eliminates the scrubbing factor of wild grasses which contain field runoff until broken down.

Fencing protects against free-roaming cattle which trample stream banks increasing siltation and widening the stream. Riffles are covered with mud and a wide stream slows the current. Water warms and the stream no longer has the velocity to cleanse itself.

Stream rehabilitation is the most expensive means of extending quality trout water but it is by any measure the best way to improve trout populations. The DNR annually improves from 25 to 30 miles of trout streams with a majority of the effort occuring southeast.

Thanks to the $5 Minnesota trout stamp, about $175,000 is allocated annually (trout stamps have levelled off at 100,000 a year) for stream improvements. The chief limiting factor is cost of staff.

Stream improvements are wide-ranging: crib shelters are box-like affairs constructed in the stream (or pre-fabbed) generally on the outside bend of a pool. Topped with riprap, soil and vegetation, they serve as 'deluxe' undercut banks - perfect lairs for lunker trout. A good crib is not noticeable yet good fishermen will sense their presence.

16

Current deflectors direct the current into a strategic area (say a root wad), scouring out the bottom where trout might want to hold on a current edge. Often constructed in conjunction with a deeper crib shelter, they provide a feeding station where trout may remain in slower-moving water while perusing the menu available in faster water.

This is prime habitat. The water is cool and the trout can hide easily.

Eroded banks signal slow-moving warm water and few fish.

17

Channel narrowing concentrates water flow, cooling the stream and exposing gravel and rock substrate which submerged vegetation and aquatic insects then colonize.

Small waterfalls - 'tumbler logs' - create "plunge pools" below the logs where trout can congregate.

The Root River

The Root River South Branch, Fillmore County, is the largest (21 miles) stream system rated "good" trout habitat. The South Branch is as popular and easy to fish as any stream in the state. The 10 miles from Forestville State Park to Preston is heavily fished (2,000 hrs. per mile) with opening day crowds literally shoulder to shoulder from the park to Carimona.

Alas, much of the stream bank has eroded and sloughed into the river drowning riffles and eliminating overhangs. Pools are large but slow-moving with very little cover. Chubs, suckers and a few 10" trout scurry from pool to pool in frantic and futile effort to hide. This is poor fish habitat but, like lakeshore, easily fishable.

Surveying the carnage wrought by abuse of the watershed, one feels like a spectator in the Roman Colosseum. In order to satisfy demand, catchable fish are stocked in these clear-water amphitheaters. Their life expectancy is about that of a gladiator facing a pride of hungry lions armed with a vulcanized sword.

On the other hand, one has only to try the mile of totally rehabilitated Root River within Forestville State Park to experience firsthand what heaven is like for a trout angler.

Here, virtually every foot of stream has been cultivated in a divine experiment geared to achieve maximum habitat. Eroded banks have been shored up with limestone riprap, flow pooled beneath tumbler logs and water deflected to produce perfect lies. Even a mediocre fisherman can get 20 takes in a couple hours of fishing.

An acquaintance fishing this stretch reported getting strikes on two dozen consecutive casts, landing six fish over 5 lbs., being broken off three times by larger fish and detecting a pick-up over 200 times - all in a single, arm-deadening day. This is prime water where a 15" fish (4 yrs. old) is considered small.

18

This 'miracle mile' of course, is catch-and-release artificials only, but it gives a glimpse of enlightened resource management. Do yourself a favor and try it, and remember to pinch down those barbs. The park has 60 campsites but fills on weekends so call ahead or arrive early.

Beaver Creek

Another area boasting stream improvements - and excellent natural reproduction of native browns - while allowing anglers to creel fish during the regular season, is Beaver Creek.

Beaver Creek has been lucky in that the eastern arm of the Creek is substantially contained within Beaver Creek Valley State Park with minimal agricultural impact on the stream itself. While the flat areas above the valley are farmed, the slopes remain a northern hardwood and oak community interspersed with thick growth of native prairie. Despite the potential for flooding, the stream is in remarkably good condition with a minimum of mud filling in the deeper holes where trout prosper.

Beaver Creek is trophy brown trout water where the angler is advised to use stealth and a large (size #2) hook. These fish bare little resemblance to their hatchery cousins and are noted for their tenacity. Woe to any angler who fails to make a good hook set before he begins to ladle on the butter!

Whitewater River

The Whitewater River - Main, Middle, North and South Branches - make up half of the 40 miles in Winona County rated "good" for stream trout.

Recent flooding (1988-89) wiped out most natural reproduction and caused the system to fall back on infusions of thousands of hatchery rainbows and browns. While hatchery-bred fingerlings are not first choice among DNR professionals and experienced fly-fishermen, they do provide a democratic angling experience and bolster reproductive stock.

Whitewater State Park, located on State Highway 74 between St. Charles and Elba, has many suitable trout lies within it although upstream erosion has left mud and warmer water in place of once magnificent brook trout habitat.

The confluence of the Middle Branch and a short section of stream known as Trout Run (not to be confused with Trout Run Creek) occurs within the park and is as good a place as any to begin. I've always caught or seen fish here and have had a few break 4# tippets. This is the "old" section of the park which once hosted numerous campsites but, as attested by the forest reclamation of the adjacent golf course, was too costly and perilous to maintain in the face of incessant flooding.

Directly behind the new Cedar Hill Campground and for several hundred yards downstream are a series of fine riffles where hungry trout can be heard feeding at dawn or dusk; these fish are smaller, from 10-12" but don't lack for aggressiveness.

Nearby Elba (pop. 200) offers two additional venues for exploration: a) Route 25, a dirt road running northwest out of town shadows the North Branch and offers fair trout habitat; b) County Rd. 26 runs east out of town one mile before turning south on unimproved 37. There are two entry points off of this road.

The first is some 500' before the bridge. Deadfalls and gravel bars in this area make for easy stalking and large fish. I once saw a dozen trout in the 2# range form a tight group in the middle of the current below the bridge. They weren't taking during midday but others were — on hellgrammite and grasshopper imitations. The bridge is some 50 yards downstream from the 48 degree outflow of the Crystal Springs Trout Hatchery.

About a half-mile above the hatchery the road dead ends at an abandoned bridge. Below the bridge and for a mile upstream the dedicated angler has a wide selection of delicious trout haunts to cast to. This section is under special regulations requiring artificials only with all fish caught to be released.

To catch mammoth trout, one should return to Elba. Below the town, the three branches commingle into a slow-moving, twisting tangle of a river contemptuous of the fisherman's preference for solid footing and picturesque presentation. (Also try the South Fork Root River below Beaver Creek near the town of Houston.)

There are fewer fish in this warm water but they are apt to be summa cum laude graduates of Jungle 'U'; in this corner are fish who regard hatchery products as breakfast. If you want to fish here, put away the fly-rod and grab the spinning rig, tie a large sinking rapala on the end of 10# test and put a flashlight in your lunch bucket.

The state record brown is 16 lbs. and came out of Grindstone Lake — a lake by god! While no Flaming Gorge by any means, a 16 lb. brown spells trouble.

Southeast waters - already yielding fish of 13 (Trout Run Creek, near Troy) and 14 lbs. (Whitewater) - are the last hope of restoring integrity to the stream angler. In fact, a local resident claims to have seen a really big trout - a really big trout, some three feet long (!) - dining on a family of muskrats. If it weren't for young children at home, I would track the beast myself.

Using a DNR guide "Trout Streams of Southeast Minnesota," a state highway map, and advice and directions from local fly shops, gas station attendants or State Park personnel, it's easy to have a major ecstatic trout fishing experience.

A favorite tactic is to arrive before or after the weekend and drive country roads paralleling the streams. Check out the many paths worn from the highway or hone your sortie toward a parked vehicle belonging (you hope) to a local. Bon Voyage!

And a Waterhole

As for watering holes, my favorite has always been Mauer Bros. in Elba. A family operation for over 100 years, the saloon has weathered floods, prohibition, motorcycle gangs, yuppies and hair loss.

The later was perhaps the most severe challenge of all. Nicholas Mauer, says son John, began collecting stuffed animals soon after his return from WWI. Eventually, Nicholas' pastime became an obsession, and by the 1960's the bar's walls were festooned with all manner of furred creatures, some rightfully suspected of other-worldly origins.

With the years, the taxidermist's skills disappeared under a layer of soot and smoke; even the pure white coat of the ermine came to look like a deckhand on the Exxon Valdez. During cleaning, various animal pelts exited down the vacuum cleaner, says Mike Mauer, Nicholas' grandson and current co-owner with brother Jim.

A new menagerie is now taking shape but a treasury of memories remain including exhibits of the largest trout ever taken from local waters. Mauer Bros. hosts an annual summer-long trout-fishing contest and a prominent honor roll of weekly winners makes for interesting reading.

Chapter 2

Metro

Here, There
and Everywhere

To catch a fish it is necessary to know where the fish is — or is not. This will save hours of plying "empty" waters. While sport is the heart of fishing, geography is its mind. Fish think with their stomachs, generally confining their feeding movements to the littoral area, or that part of the lake 15' or less in depth. With the latest space-age paraphernalia, it is quite possible to cover every inch of productive water in a few hours.

In order to keep pace with fish-catching technology, Minnesota's fish experts in the Department of Natural Resources resort to the latest in fish-managing science. "Sometimes fishermen think that every lake can be managed to produce every fish in good size and vast numbers, but it's simply not possible on a take-out basis," warns Duane Shodeen, metro area fisheries supervisor.

Shodeen oversees the 200 plus lakes of the 7-county metro area that are deemed fishable. It's an occasionally onerous task since 700,000 license holders come with the territory and one- sixth of all angling trips in the state occur right here.

"We can plant only so many fish per acre of littoral - at the edge of carrying capacity - but where we cannot control the harvest, we cannot produce numerous fish." Shodeen doesn't advocate skipping a fish meal altogether, but he does counsel a certain amount of savvy: "Do you want to take the kids out for some fast action - we have plenty of lakes with smaller fish - or do you want to wait for a lunker?"

Every lake has its own character maintains Shodeen, and careful reading of the DNR's computerized survey of each of the state's lakes can determine subtle ecological relationships in the piscine environment which can maximize time spent on the water.

If that sounds a bit arcane, listen as Shodeen and Bruce Gilbertson, area fisheries supervisor, provide a species primer for local enthusiasts. And if you pay close attention to the swirls and eddies of their conversation, you may just hook onto locations insiders would never breathe.

Panfish — "80% of all fish harvested in the metro area are sunfish and crappies," begins Shodeen, himself a panfishing connoisseur. Since these morsels are relatively easy to apprehend, they're "fished hard, cropped heavily"; the aim of DNR management is to increase the number of 6" fish which fishermen creel.

To accomplish this, Fisheries technologists have to deal with a population crisis: without an efficient predator to crop sunfish hatches, a lake will produce an overabundance of first-year 2" sunnies; these tiny, quick-moving fish will snap up available aquatic insects before the slower 3-4" fish can move in. Because fishermen do not creel these latter sizes, the entire population is fated to slow growth.

The solution, for sunfish and bluegills at least (crappies are another story), lies with the largemouth bass. But not just any largemouth, it must be a particular size as well.

Largemouth Bass — The largemouth is an extremely efficient sunfish predator consuming fish 1/4 its size as its preferred diet. Adjusting to this predilection, Shodeen explains, DNR strategy introduces 8" bass fingerlings to feed on the hordes of first-year sunnies.

Also, by placing a slot limit of 12-16" on bass, that portion of bass which most directly impacts overabundant bluegills can be protected. Above and below the limit (an 18" bass may weigh 3 1/2 pounds) fish may be creeled. Meanwhile, surviving 2" panfish rapidly become 3-4" fish in their second year, and harvestable 5-6"ers in their third.

Supporting Shodeen's theory is experience in southern reservoirs subjected to five times the fishing pressure of our northern lakes. There, bass and sunfish do well together (given equal fishing pressure), with a whopping 20-40% of sunfish reaching 6" as opposed to the 1% Shodeen cites for the metro area.

Furthermore, were bass to benefit from catch and release, stricter possession limits (now six daily), and the elimination of predators, the day of 6,8, and even 10 pounders becoming common in Minnesota lakes would be right around the dock.

Walleye — In deference to Minnesota's favorite fish, 94% of the 375 million fry and fingerlings stocked annually in state's public waters are walleye. Some quarter-million of these are planted in metro lakes which long ago lost natural spawning areas to the demands of urban living.

In Minneapolis, 2,000 fingerlings are apportioned to Nokomis and 6,900 to Calhoun every other year. The reason for the alteration in year classes is evidence that the closer in size walleye classes are, the more they compete for food thus slowing their growth. Proof that first and third year fish aren't competitors is found in repeated catches of 4-5 pound fish in city lakes.

Muskellunge — Muskie hybrids (male pike/female muskellunge) are a fairly recent addition to metro fishing excitement. This fast-growing giant has been stocked in the lake chains of both Minneapolis and St. Paul.

A 33 lb. hybrid muskie was taken from Lake Calhoun in August, 1991; a 27 lb. pure-bred Leech Lake strain was caught and released on Harriet in 1986. Lake Rebecca, near Rockford, is said to be an excellent muskie location; with a ban on all but electric motors, it is quiet as well.

Northern Pike — If you are looking for trophy northern - fish in the 20 pound class - do not go to a lake drained by several seasonally-flooded marshes, says Gilbertson. "This kind of habitat makes for excellent pike spawning, and the biggest determinant in the growth rate of any species is its ability to get off successive good hatches. If the pike fry get decent initial growth, they will impact the food supply in such a way that their future growth will be affected — you'll get hammer-handles."

Gilbertson qualifies this as relatively recent knowledge: "We didn't know this could happen to predator fish. We knew a given lake could only produce so many fish; we didn't know that most predator fish - northern, walleye, muskie and bass -

can become so abundant that their average growth rate drops drastically."

The large number of northerns compete with each other so successfully, explains Gilbertson, that perch, the main forage fish for northern, are reduced to very low levels. "When the perch are gone, pike will feed on walleye fingerlings because their bullet shape is similar to the perch which the pike are conditioned to feed upon. Pike are reluctant to feed on crappies and bluegills because their shape is more difficult to swallow."

To prove the point, Gilbertson recalls the work which turned Lake Harriet into a muskie hot spot: First, a natural spawning area on the northeast side of the lake was removed. Pike were then removed annually to give the young muskie fingerlings a chance.

The first year of removal, 700 small pike (average size for Harriet northerns at the time was 1 to 1 1/2 pounds) were netted. Subsequent seinings revealed fewer small pike, more large ones. "After five years," according to Gilbertson, "the average pike netted was 10 pounds — forage base perch had exploded!"

Lakes managed for trophy-sized experiences with pike or hybrid muskie include Cedar Lake in Scott County ("good numbers of fish in the 12-20 pound range") and the Twin Cities lake chains.

For younger anglers who may not appreciate a sporting encounter with a thrashing behemoth, smaller pike may be found in White Bear Lake ("probably a few 20 pounders but they're overwhelmed by smaller sized fish") and Lake Minnewashta in Carver County.

Fall Turnover

November in Minnesota marks the period of fall turnover when water temperature and oxygen supply equalize throughout a lake. This means that structure loses significance in terms of fish location as fish can find ideal, that is, similar, conditions just about anywhere. They no longer relate to structure in the same way and scatter top to bottom in search of food for the approaching winter.

As cold-blooded creatures, the onset of frosty temperatures sparks increased activity after the lethargy of summer, and the general availability of oxygen means short bursts of speed needed to seize prey can readily be accommodated.

Nor is the thermocline - that area of interface between warmer, lighter surface water and colder, denser bottom water where fish are often found during summer - much of a factor since lake mixing has made it temporarily disappear. Also, water clarity which increases in early fall as algae and weeds slow their growth, suddenly decreases in late fall as surface winds easily mix water layers of equal density. This means predators can remain in shallow water longer without giving in to fear of detection.

Until surface water temp drops low enough to freeze, fish need not go deep for warmer water but can find it and food in the shallows where they are likely to remain until freeze-up.

For female fish which give up a large portion of their weight for egg production over the winter, this is the time of their lives. Anything and everything that wiggles, twitches or skitters in or on the lake will be engulfed, inhaled, consumed and otherwise converted to piscine protein.

Curiously, this is also the time that the lake's largest and most unpredictable predator - homo rodreelus - makes his exit. Something to do with stiffness in the joints or couchitis apparently. 'Tis a pity for fall, like spring, is an occasion for lunker catches and, furthermore, it's easy.

You don't have to chase the fish as in trolling, or pull out the electronic gear, the boat, etc. to find the perfect spot. In fact, the fish will come to you. All you have to do is find the shoreline and, unlike other times of the year when weeds get in your way, now they are the way.

Weeds grow best in shallow areas of the lake and it is these areas that in the fall hold the best chance to catch fish. Shallow waters warm more quickly on sunny days and they house the lion's share of phytoplankton, zooplankton and minnows which are the essential early links of the aquatic food chain. The beauty of fishing shallow weeds beds is that you do not need a boat. A 7-7 1/2' graphite casting rod and 6-8# mono with advanced casting capability like Prime or TriMax, will put even a light floating plug 100' from shore.

And a big (6-7") jointed floating plug is recommended for fall behemoths. The plug doesn't get caught in the weeds and, on a calm morning or evening, its sensual impulses casts a vast net over the weed tops. Methodical casting and reeling may work but the most productive measures involve a patient retrieve filled with all sort of erratic twitches, 30 second stops and short tugs left and right causing the plug to act like a floundering minnow.

If you have a few feet of water over the weed tops, you may try a neutrally buoyant plug which can be made to sink or rise with a flick of the wrist. These doctored plugs begin life as floaters but with the addition of lead tape or split shot embedded in the front of the lure, floatation is overcome and the lure sinks ever so slowly. With a twitch of the rod tip it rises like a wounded minnow to the surface only to submerge again with tantalizing vulnerability.

Spoons work too but are less versatile since they must be retrieved quickly in order to avoid weeds and can't be used at night when fall fishing is hottest. Fishing with live minnows also faces limitations at this time because it is imperative to stay near the weeds where the big ones are and yet live bait has a tendency to hide in the weeds if given enough slack.

Be sure to use a wire leader as northern pike are especially active this time of year and the bigger they are the more teeth they have. A pair of fingerless wool gloves will keep hands warm and fingers functioning. And bring a large landing net; my last pike was too big for the average-sized net, dropped out and swam away.

Ice Fishing for Panfish

Ice fishing has three seasons: December, when fish are shallow and somewhat active; January, when fish metabolism slows as the ice grows; and February/March, as blue ice and procreative instincts combine for exciting angling. Real icefishermen don't fish December; December is the month tourists from Samoa slide cautiously onto the ice to have their pictures taken. Real ice fishermen wait for January.

January demands peak readiness by way of technique and equipment. Fish are deeper. The aquatic environment is darker thanks to snow piled on the ice. Water temperatures are near freezing. And a full schedule of ice fishing contests have left *piscinus no sleepous* searching for thorazine rather than baitfish.

29

But the fish are still there. In fact, DNR sources say more fish are caught during winter than any other season. You will need a little something extra, however.

If you decide to take up the challenge offered by an ill-tempered Mother Nature, you will certainly want an ice house. Whether or not you want to purchase a semi-portable 1 or 2 person shelter for $100-$200 is another question. Permanent ice houses may be rented by the day, week or month on the more popular lakes. Even an unheated ice shack can add 25 degrees of warmth.

Ice fishing rituals, here on Forest Lake circa 1940's, are as old as the Druids.

If you choose to forgo the comfort of a total environment, give some thought to a propane tank and heating coil ($70), particularly on those days when an 'Alberta Clipper' - known to single out ice fishermen for special attention - is in the vicinity.

On warmer days, one might get by sitting on an empty 5-gallon pail with a patch of carpet under the feet. Since ice reflects rather than absorbs sunlight, that is, allows potentially warming rays to bounce back into space rather than traps them, most open areas can be expected to lend new insight into the term hypothermia.

Even if just going out to see what those strange folk are doing, remember "wooldownfelt." That is, wool stocking cap or balaclava; down vest for the torso (re: heart); and felt-lined rubberized boots (Sorels, $55-65). Chopper-type leather mittens with fleece linings ($15) are a necessity for outdoor fishing in January — no stylish leather gloves, please. A flask-like hand warmer powered by lighter fluid is a good idea for a quick Rx on numb fingertips.

Suppose you haven't been talked into watching televised golf and still want to ice a line: you'll need an ice auger.

It's a choice of money vs. muscle: a power auger costs $200 and will penetrate 20" of ice in 30 seconds; a manual auger costs only $25 and is guaranteed to heat you up beyond the 2-5 minutes exertion each new hole requires.

The 7" size is recommended, especially on the manual type. An ice scoop ($5) to keep ice from re-forming in the hole is a cool investment. With your last fin you can get a small ice rod, ice flies and some live grubs.

For panfish, use a short, stiff rod with a flexible tip often called a "jiggle stick." This could be a simple rod with pegs to store 60' of 2-4# monofilament line or a more versatile outfit with a reel to store line or even to play fish. A panfish set-up of this design shouldn't cost more than $10.

Where to find the fish and how to rig up: sunfish and crappies will generally be found in water 10'-20' deep. Perch may be deeper, to 30'. With the exception of crappie schools suspended over deep water in mid-lake, most panfish relate to shoreline vegetation and can be picked up within 100' of the beach.

Topographic maps can be useful in this regard and will save the expense of a flasher depth finder. Depth can also be determined by adding a clip-on sinker to the line and dropping it to the bottom.

Look on the topo map for points that extend into the lake, channels between lakes or bays, and weedy areas near drop-offs to deeper water. Because there is no wave action under the ice, zooplankton and other prey of minnows and thus panfish, is evenly distributed through the littoral area. The fish will be spread out therefore, and it may take more than one hole to locate them. Stay near weedy cover.

31

While the types and styles of ice-flies and tear-drop jigs are nearly endless, a personal favorite is a single hook fastened by means of split-ring to a 1" blaze orange or chartreuse Swedish Pimple. A single hook allows quicker release of a hooked fish: the hands are less exposed, the bait can be returned to the water faster and unwanted fish can removed alive.

Add some small plastic flipper in yellow or red to the split-ring to attract attention, or thread a colorful glass bead on the line in front of the lure. Alternatives to the Pimple include a pink and yellow marabou (feathered) jig and plastic tube jigs.

Tip the hook with several insect larvae: colored eurolarvae or "maggies," are preferred; wax worms are also good. The flash of the Pimple and the action of the flippers, feathers or plastic will attract fish, but it is the worm which triggers the strike.

Some fishermen use split-shot to get the lure down faster, others like bobbers on the line to indicate strikes and return the lure to the desired depth. It's a matter of preference. Many anglers maintain bobbers freeze in the hole, get in the way and, like split-shot, lessen sensitivity.

Because sensitivity is so important in January when hits can be more subtle than an Agatha Christie novel, a spring-bobber is highly recommended. This simple device consists of a sliver of steel bent at an angle from the rod tip to which it is affixed. The line extends through an eyelet on the device and, when the rod is held still, conveys to the eye, the slightest mouthing of the bait below. This brings us to the action the angler wants to impart to the bait to trigger the strike.

Jig the lure by dropping it to the bottom and reeling in 6-8". Now lift the rod tip up that same 6-8" with a slight snap of the wrist and let it fall back again keeping a tight line. Pause a few seconds and repeat. That's all there is to it.

If you find little action after 5 minutes, move upward 6" or 1' in the water column and keep doing so until you find fish or decide to move to a different location. Big fish are often found on or near the bottom in winter, or at least circling below smaller fish.

Since the strike generally comes as the lure flutters downward, vary the rhythm of your presentation either by jigging in larger increments - 1' or 1.5' instead of 6" - or by jigging the bait rapidly several times in succession before pausing.

Sunfish can be nabbed anytime during the day but seldom bite at night. Crappies often bite best in low-light conditions and are dependable nocturnal feeders. Sunnies stick to the top of weedbeds while crappies move about in the water column and in the latter part of the season may be found directly under the ice.

Remember that crappies are a schooling fish and class moves about every 15 minutes. When you find either species, there should be plenty of action, at least for a while. Good sized panfish, from 3/4 to 1# can be found in larger waters such as Lake Minnetonka or the Mississippi River backwaters near Winona.

Two lines are allowed per license in winter and, if you do get a shelter, it requires an annual permit. A final admonition: leave the booze at home (alcohol contributes to heat loss) in favor of a thermos of hot apple cider.

Ice Fishing for the Big Ones

Larger fish such as walleye and northern typically demand larger artillery by way of tackle, but not as large as you might think. Since waters are clearer in the winter stillness than they are in summer, and because the lure does not move as fast, fish have more time to notice such details as painted eyes and steel meat-hooks.

It's a time for subtlety; the lure is generally fished where it is darkest - a foot off the bottom or the top of weed beds; live bait is always preferred; a stinger hook comes in very handy on the hookset for these sluggish giants.

Walleyes will inhabit deeper water, to 40'. They will maneuver over bottom topography between resting and feeding stations seeking out stair-like progressions from deep to shallow water; relatively gradual progressions (2-5') are best.

Sharp drop-offs from the littoral area (where weeds receive sufficient light to grow) to deep water, do not offer the predator the comfort of relating to the bottom that gradual shoreline breaks do.

Fish prefer these step-like slopes and will congregate below such ladders (inside break), and at their tops where the first descent occurs between shoreline and deeper water (outside break). Sandbars, sunken islands, small rock piles and outlets to other bodies of water near such stairways are the first places to look. Check out any shoreline point eliminating possibilities with a topographic map.

Northerns will be shallower, often to five feet in or over thick weeds. A 5-7" minnow or part of minnow on a jigging spoon is best. A wire leader and 10-12# mono makes sense on these dental dandies.

Contraptions designed for jigging include side-planing lures which move laterally in a wide arc thus attracting fish from a large area, and jigging spoons which tumble irregularly flashing a polished or painted surface to entice a strike.

Among the side-planers are the Jigging Rapala, a minnow imitation with single hooks at either end and fins to push it horizontally, and the airplane jig with wings to swim it in a zig-zag pattern. The airplane jig can be lifted 5-10" with a light-action spinning rod; the higher the lift, the further the drift.

Jigging spoons rely on flash and erratic action. They come in polished silver, gold, and copper, or painted in bright fluorescent or glowing phosphorescent colors. Polished metal and fluorescence depend on some light for their effectiveness; phosphorescence (and chemical luminescence) work at depth where there is little or no light.

Phosphorescence requires the lure be 'augmented' every few minutes by a light source, whether a flashlight or a small battery-powered camera flash unit. Examples of jigging spoons are the Rocker Minnow, Salty Dog, Swedish Pimple and Walleye Hawger.

Jigging spoons tumble best on a slack line. To fish a spoon, lift the rod tip up at least 2', the let it drop. Don't be reluctant to start on the bottom. Not only do large predators seem to prefer the bottom in winter, but the disturbance caused by the spoon slapping the bottom just may bring in fish attracted by plumes of dirt.

Pause a second or two once the line is still. Make the pause definite since this is when a strike is likely to occur. Always be prepared for a tug after a pause.

When you feel a fish, try not to pull directly upward on the hookset because this will draw the hook toward the hard bony plate on top of the mouth. Instead, set the hook at an angle, embedding it in the soft side of the mouth.

This brings up the importance of a 'stinger' hook. A stinger is a second hook tied by means of a 2-3" piece of mono behind the main hook.

Stingers are important because of the way predator fish eat. After sizing up the prey, a big fish will grab it at right angles and swim with it a few feet. Then it will release the prey and grab it again in a series of quick bites. These maneuvers re-position the predator's jaws until the prey can be swallowed head first so the victim's dorsal fin does not get caught in the aggressor's throat.

The entire sequence may happen in an eyelash; large predators are well practiced—they've been doing this to smaller fish since they were barely visible slivers 1/2" long.

Such a method of attack often means that on the first rush the pike has not encountered the hook at all. If you attempt to set the hook on this initial hit, you may simply force a tug-of-war for the bait.

You are likely to "win" this contest when the fish sees the hole and lets go. A second hook placed in the side of the bait behind the dorsal fin and pointing forward can be set on the first rush if the fisherman remembers to pull sideways on the line.

Tandem hooks, the so-called "quick-strike" rig popularized by the Lindner Bros., serve a similar purpose: they catch more fish and, by not allowing the fish to swallow the hook, they permit the fisherman to release unharmed a portion of their catch.

Every fisherman to a degree related to their abilities should practice catch-and-release in order to keep the resource healthy. By removing factory trebles and substituting single hooks attached 2-3" apart with heavy-duty mono or wire, the fisherman can save more fish and keep the "sport" in sportfishing.

Bass Tournament Veteran
Offers Insight

Bill Niccum has been fishing large mouth bass all of his life, first with his father and then with his own boat on Lake Minnetonka where he owns and operates Minnetonka Portable Dredging.

He got pretty good at it too, searching out the coontail weeds where ol' bucketmouth resides, flipp'n his preferred jig-n- pig to the weedline, keeping a tight line while the bait fell, staying alert for the slight hesitation that signals a pick-up and hitting the rod hard in order to set the hook while *micropterus salmoides lacepede* bucked and twisted like a locomotive tumbling down a mountainside. Then, a few years back, he decided to test himself on the tournament trail.

"I started on the Great Plains circuit (no longer around) which held five tournaments in Minnesota to qualify for the Superstar Nationals. You had to be in the top 10 and I qualified all four years I entered. Sometimes I'd be going to 25-30 tournaments a year; it got to where the business suffered.

"But I really enjoyed it. My wife, Judy, would come along and we'd socialize after the fishing. The best part of tournament fishing was the people we met."

The worst part of tournament fishing, says Niccum, was the pressure. "It's a competition, there's pressure each minute when you're trying to catch fish, a certain fish, certain hours, on certain days."

It wasn't only the pressure that took some of the shine off the tournament experience either, according to Niccum. "We usually weren't catching big bass. When you've got 100 boats out there speeding around, the fish seem to get smarter, schools scatter and the big ones disappear. Tournament day is difficult; sometimes 3-4 fish might win."

Niccum's five-pounders pre-release somewhere in western Hennepin County.

Niccum never won the draw, or individual part of the tournament, but neither did he finish far back. "I got a lot of second places and won some of the team competitions, as well as a couple money pots for the largest fish. It's often just a matter of luck; many times I caught a fish that put me in the money on my last cast."

Niccum's strategy began with the typical pre-tournament fishing day: "When the tournament began, you'd go after those fish you caught the day before, shallow or deep, it didn't matter."

He was well-armed: "I'd have at least five rods, sometimes 10, ready to go with different weight lines, different rigs - crankbaits, spinnerbaits, plastic worms, the jig-n-pig - different sizes. Of course, all tournaments are artificial bait only."

The prize money was never his incentive, says Niccum, "It costs $50-$75 to enter (up to $350 for a national) and first is a guaranteed $2,000 generally, but after that the money drops off pretty fast: $500 for second, $200 for third. "It really helps if you can concentrate on the sport full time; it makes a difference. Some people live for it, they're real professionals. I love bass, I grew up fishing them and I've never fished anything else."

Despite his life-long interest and tournament experience, Niccum rarely kills a bass. "Tournaments don't harm the fishery much anymore. When I started there was a 2 oz. deduction for each dead fish, now the standard penalty is half the weight for a dead fish. Mortality is low, 99% go back alive. The worst I ever saw was a tournament on Minnetonka with real hot weather and amateurs mishandling some of the fish. Even then, I'd estimate only 10% were lost; they had to be eaten, unfortunately."

Niccum plans to cut back on his tournament entries these days, concentrating on the Minnetonka Classic and "maybe one or two others" but he won't lack for memories. His best weight was on Clearwater Lake near Annandale, when he recorded 10 fish for 33 lbs. The "most thrilling" was a tournament where he caught 9 fish in the last 10 minutes — including the "hog" of the tournament on his last cast.

Plus, he's fished famed bass waters all over the country, including Bull Shoals, Ark., Lake O' The Cherokees, Okla., and Lake of The Ozarks, Mo. He's even fished bass reservoirs in Cuba. "Now, where else but bass fishing," concludes Niccum, "can you have so much fun — and all after you're forty, too?"

Animal Nuisance Part of Suburban Lifestyle

Deer running down Main Street, wild turkeys roosting in the backyard, snakes wintering in the basement — no, not likely in a downtown condo but almost routine in suburban areas as residential uses invade the formerly wild environs of the Twin Cities.

Beaver, raccoons, muskrats, woodchucks, skunks, squirrels, etc., are still under the impression that the outdoors belongs to them. This attitude is tested daily in western Hennepin County according to Mitch Schneider, Animal Control Officer for Eden Prairie. "We get hundreds of calls annually and we always will because the city's planned development includes a great deal of wildlife."

Each municipality in the area is apt to pursue its own unique policy in dealing with animal-human encounters of the annoying kind but, in general, none allow the discharge of firearms within the city and most discourage use of leg-hold traps to deal with the wild intruder. "It usually depends on the nature of the complaint," says Schneider, a man who obviously has not let work rob him of his sense of humor.

"We contact the DNR if the animal is large and difficult to live-trap like the beaver. Fortunately, we get few beaver complaints but they can be very destructive, either by chewing on trees or damming up small streams and creating flooded basements.

"Property owners have the right to trap but, again, they have to get a permit from the DNR and we discourage use of leg-hold traps because they can endanger children and domestic pets.

"If the call is about an animal which is not causing damage or attacking a family pet, but is simply being noisy, we suggest other measures. For instance, if it's a beaver that may chew on trees we recommend putting chicken wire around the trunk to a height of 3'; beaver will normally not go to the trouble of gnawing on a protected trunk if others are available."

As for dealing with most critters, Eden Prairie has a particularly novel approach: "We live-trap them and move them to a farm the city owns on Highway 5," says Schneider, "there we release the animal and say, 'Shoo, go to Chanhassen.'"

Some creatures however, face a different fate according to Schneider: "Because of the high percentage of rabidity in skunks, we live-trap them, cover them with a cloth so they don't spray and then dispatch them by drowning."

Live-trapping too, has its drawbacks DNR personnel admit. Animals caught in a live-trap may suffer high mortality because of the stress involved in confinement. There is also the problem of where to put the beast?

Animals which come into conflict with humans are often forced into such interaction because of over-population in their normal range, says DNR Conservation Officer Jim Konrad. "Lack of food or territory alone creates stress and as a result these creatures are susceptible to diseases such as round worm or the distemper complex which wouldn't affect a healthy animal.

"Releasing them in new territory where they don't know how to locate food and shelter sources means you're probably killing it anyway. Except now you might be adding disease to a healthy population as well."

Konrad says the DNR proposes that if an animal is to be trapped it should be destroyed. The DNR allows leg-hold traps to collect nuisance animals during the appropriate season, using licensed trappers who do the job and collect compensation from the value of the pelt.

This policy works well with most fur-bearers. However, in the case of beaver, it runs into problems because of the current low demand for beaver pelts and the difficulty a 50 lb. animal can create.

Outside the Twin Cities, the DNR has additional management techniques, since statute allows a property owner to shoot an animal on sight if the animal is damaging property. The only requirement is that the carcass of the animal thus "terminated with extreme prejudice" be turned over to the DNR within 48 hours.

Within the metro area, where hunting and trapping are "pre-empted" by city officials, the DNR does not like to become involved. "It gets very complicated," says Konrad, "when you're dealing with municipalities that have no animal control options, or that take care of problems with dogs and cats but not wild animals."

For this reason, the DNR offers preventive advice in several pamphlets available to the public.

"In the case of raccoons which are the single most frequent complaint, we tell the homeowner to keep their garbage cans inside the garage until collection day."

Collection day is nearly every day in the case of Minnetonka's springtime raccoon problem says Jean Long, Animal Control Officer for that city. "Spring is nesting time for raccoons and they seem particularly fond of chimneys. They can really make a mess.

"First, the mother raccoon pulls out her fur to make a nest, then there is the urine and droppings which make their way to the ground floor fireplace." Raccoons, says Long, also travel with their own retinue: fleas and mice.

(Nor is the problem completely suburban: a resident of Uptown, Minneapolis, recently learned not to put corncobs - favorite salad ingredient of raccoons - into their compost heap. And a homeowner near West River Rd. it's been reported, is placing plastic caps over her basement window wells after being attacked by a female raccoon whose nesting preparations included plugging the clothes dryer exhaust.)

Long currently logs 5-7 calls a week concerning raccoons and wishes to pass on this advice: "Take the time to place a wire barrier over the chimney and check eaves to close openings there since raccoons also like to nest next to the masterbedroom for some reason." That is, if they can move in before the squirrels do.

This warning can be ignored only at great peril and expense says Long. Not only because Minnetonka is "real woodsy" but also because once afflicted, homeowners will have to rent their own live-traps or face expensive treatment from a qualified chimney sweep. Long would like to point out too, that basement window wells make splendid nurseries for skunks.

Minnetonka destroys its nuisance animals according to Long, unless they are rare. She has so far encountered a "hairless" raccoon, an opossum, and the infrequently-sighted spotted skunk.

Obviously, an ounce of chicken wire is worth several pounds of startled skunk — especially for the animal doomed to be designated a "nuisance". Remember the words of the DNR's Konrad and prepare: "Let's face it, the reality of living in the woods is animal interaction."

What's Going On
With Our Lakes?

The world's supply of water - that bluegreen solvent called upon to bathe away the sweat and sooth the thirst of billions - is limited. Only 369,820,250,000,000,000,000 gallons. Sounds safe even in a dry July. But 369 quintillion, 820 quadrillion, 250 trillion is a drop misleading.

Actually, 97.3 % of all water is not freshwater; it's saltwater, part of the world's oceans. The 2.7 % remaining, or 10 quintillion gallons, is freshwater, available to the international multitudes. But that's not quite as its sounds either because 77% of the 10 quintillion - enough to fill the Mississippi's thirst for 50,000 years - is frozen. Yes, the polar ice caps.

The flat truth of the matter is that of our remaining 20 %, 2/3's locked in stone 2,500 feet beneath the earth.

If you care to count the amount of fresh water tied up in the atmosphere, a meager .04 %, that leaves a surprisingly small figure - .35 % - found in our lakes and swamps. Small as it is, this figure is of a very high order in the land we occupy as Minnesotans.

The lakes of the state comprise most of the area's beauty and all of its spirit. Freshwater lakes and wetlands bind the land to the skies, and the people to each other by way of a common language of fishing, swimming, boating, and just plain sitting in awed silence at the grandeur of moving water.

Lake Types

For those of us who have visited a goodly number of Minnesota's bounty, all freshwater is not alike. All lakes are pretty but some's prettier than others, as the saying goes. Unfortunately, the prettiest is always the youngest, although middle-age is often the period of a lake's greatest usefulness to man while a lake's declining years serve to clean and recharge the resource.

Not surprisingly, no water is absolutely pure, picking up impurities - calcium, silica, chloride, sodium, manganese, potassium phosphate (that phosphate is a good one to remember), nitrate and iron among others - from every natural and unnatural feature it comes into contact with. However, in northeastern Minnesota, recent glaciers swept loose gravel from the landscape leaving volcanic-rock basins and deep, cold lakes with clear, infertile water.

An example of such a lake is Superior where average water temperature is 41 degrees and depth reaches a thousand feet. Despite its size, Superior contains remarkably little plant and animal life. This lack of organic matter within the lake give its waters a gem-like clarity from which there is no recovery.

These lakes are called "oligotrophic," literally "few nutrients." The fact that plants cannot grow well either on the surface of Lake Superior or its shallow areas is because several critical ingredients of plant production are missing. We can be forgiven at this point for calling these ingredients "pollution."

The chief pollutant is phosphorus. Without phosphorus, sunlight cannot convert non-living inorganic material washed into lakes by rain, winds and runoff, into living, organic plant tissue. Eventually - it should take a couple thousand years - Superior will have all the phosphorus it can handle and then some.

As phosphorus-laden bottom sediments build hundreds of feet deep and its waters warm several degrees, Superior will pass from virgin oligotrophy to a different state, that of "mesotrophy," or middle nutrients.

From a human point of view, this is the preferred lake state. Unlike the oligotrophic lake which warms in late July if at all, the mesotrophic lake is swimmable in May. This lake also has more of everything else: more fish, weeds, phosphates, sand, power boats, wind surfers, etc. Shallower water and late summer algal blooms mean certain types of fish - trout and salmon - cannot survive in such a lake but other species: bass, panfish, pike and walleye are present in great abundance.

These lakes of north central Minnesota - and Square, Christmas and Little Long lakes within the Twin Cities Metro area - are everybody's favorite owing to the warmth and productivity of their environment. But there is a third stage in the evolution of lakes which is as unsightly as it is inevitable, as annoying as it is valuable.

This is the stage of eutrophication ("well-nourished") when fertile soils and abundant minerals in the surrounding watershed dump into the lake so many nutrients that water clarity is lost, oxygen disappears from the cold-water zone, the shallows turn green and scummy with algal colonies and major shifts in species occur. Some amount of eutrophication takes place in all waters and can be beneficial from a recreational standpoint, but eventually minute changes in degree lead to major changes in quality and an accelerated state of decay - hyper-eutrophy - is reached.

Hyper-eutrophication

In the beginning, eutrophication is most marked in the epilimnion (surface waters), where increased phosphorus inputs speed up photosynthesis creating more phytoplankton, or tiny green plants. With more plant tissue to feed upon, zooplankton - microscopic floating animals (from Greek for 'wanderers') - that eat algae multiply. In turn, small minnows, and fry of gamefish, perch and sunfish, prosper feeding off these dense clusters of minute crustaceans. Larger fish consume the smaller fish and the fisherman is ready to buy a boat.

As eutrophication advances, typical mesotrophic waters move from slightly acidic (pH of 5.5-6.5) to alkaline (acid rain by contrast has a pH of 4.5). While a watery solution may be neutral at a pH of 7, many gamefish experience reproductive difficulty at pH of 8 or more. Walleye and bass eggs may not hatch but as the waters warm, their place is taken by bottom scavengers such as carp and bullheads which can tolerate higher alkalinities.

Carp feces are high in phosphorus and large populations of carp ripping up the bottom keep phosphorus available for algal use and helps push lake pH even higher. Elevated pH produces a shift in the algal community from green algae under

45

mesotrophic conditions, to the blue-green variety thanks to the latter's ability to absorb carbon dioxide and phosphate at higher pH.

While green algae are a necessary component of a rich food chain that results in powerful free-swimming predators, blue- greens are a positive nuisance. Unlike the greens which are readily digestible to zooplankton, blue-greens (those hair-like filaments which attach to rocks and docks) are poisonous to many forms of zooplankton and often kill larger animals like herons and even dogs.

Blue-greens 'blossom' along the shore and the lake becomes turbid and weedy. Hordes of stunted perch and sunfish hatch in the warm water and make use of weedy cover to escape their enemies. So many fish survive, in fact, that few grow since the small 2-3" first-year fish are faster than the older broods. These rapacious young fish swallow every zooplankton in sight and as the waters warm the zooplankton cannot make their usual daytime escape into the cooler metalimnion, or middle layer of water.

Fishermen rarely show any interest in these small fish since cleaning them is too much trouble. They toss the little ones back where they prey on the eggs and fry of the walleye and bass. Soon there are few large predators but those that do exist are quite well-fed. Someone may blame the DNR but few fathom the true nature of the changes the lake is undergoing.

As the vast blue-green algae colonies die off in the fall, the eutrophying lake becomes clear again, masking the reality of what is taking place. Meanwhile, the dead algae sinks to the bottom of the lake where it covers the sand used by the clean-water lovers - mayflies, stoneflies, dragon-fly nymphs and the like - robbing them of a home.

Poisonous gases such as hydrogen sulfide accumulate in the sediments; oxygen decreases to the point where no air-breathing fish or insect life can survive. At this point, the hypolimnion is a dark pile of rotting vegetation, an oxygen-depleted dung heap crawling with blood-red worms.

Oxygen-loving fish cannot use cooler bottom waters (now without oxygen) to escape surface water temperatures in the 70s and 80s — too hot to live. The complex ecosystem of the healthy mesotrophic lake has shifted to a simple culture which favors the growth of plant over animal life. In the end, eutrophication produces a marsh, nature's primary treatment of fouled waters.

Given the normal degree of isolation - and 10,000 years - eutrophication would overtake any lake. But Twin Cities lakes are different. They are already old. The recent glaciation which rejuvenated the lakes in the northeast, left large amounts of glacial till - sand, gravel, clay and boulders - on the metropolitan landscape.

Till provides "background" phosphorus concentrations of 20- 30 mg (ppm) per liter. Eutrophication is noticeable at levels above 20 mg according to Met Council biologist Dick Osgood, who has spent a decade studying area lakes. This means area lakes are borderline meso-eutrophic naturally. But culturally - urban culture that is - they are aging rapidly.

The Health of Area Lakes Requires Starvation

Osgood's research efforts are part of the Twin Cities Metro Area lake study (TCMA) created to provide a trophic, or nutritional, index to the area's lake resources. As it happens, there are 666 lakes larger than 25 acres within the metro area. In 1980, the Metropolitan Council was commissioned to establish a baseline data bank on priority lakes as a means of keeping track of the direction local water quality was taking.

Lakes given priority in the data bank had good recreational potential (over 100 acres with a mean depth of 10' or maximum depth of 20'); good water quality (oligotrophic or mesotrophic); or comprised a local water supply reservoir like the St. Paul lakes chain of Pleasant, Sucker, Vadnais, Peltier and Centerville.

Each of the priority lakes were exhaustively surveyed for everything from their algal populations to their fecal coliform counts. Watersheds were extensively mapped and tests conducted to determine whether heavy metals such as lead were sources of pollution. Most lakes were free of dangerous hazards to human users, but by far the most interesting data on the lakes was their relative cleanliness, or ranking on the recently devised (1977) Trophic State Index, or TSI.

The trophic status of a lake refers to the level of nutrients (from trophikos, Greek for 'nurturing') in a lake. The level of nutrients is a reliable indicator of the lake's fertility, i.e., the total quantity of plankton and nekton (fish) the body of water can support. This total quantity of life is often referred to as the lake's biomass.The fertility of a lake - the amount of biomass it produces - determines its place on the Trophic State Index.

The index ranges from 0-100 where 0-30 is oligotrophic (Exceptionally clean); 41-50 mesotrophic with Very Good water quality; from 51-70 are eutrophic conditions rated Good (50s) or Acceptable But Sometimes Unpleasant (60s); 70s are Poor; 80s Very Poor; and 90s, Severe Limitations.

It's important to remember that lakes cannot be compared as if they were all Spys, Beacons or MacIntoshes. The shape of the basin - how much is littoral area (15' deep or less) - the number of rooted plants (macrophytes), types of fish, depth, water temperature, amount of dissolved oxygen available in the hypolimnion, etc., can all play a role in determining trophic status. For example, Square Lake - an oligotrophic lake - has a similar phosphorus index as Minnetonka (upper lake), but because of its depth and spring-fed colder water less phosphorus is available for plant production.

Because of this nearly infinite variability, a single numbering system combining the three measures of total phosphorus (available nutrients), chlorophyll (actual plant growth), and secchi disk (water transparency) is used. These related indices are easily quantifiable, comprehensible to the layman and generally predictive of algal growth and thus water quality.

Trophic state is an arbitrary standard which says that each time algal biomass doubles a different trophic level is reached. Thus, total phosphorus (TP) of less than 12 micrograms per liter, chlorophyll (chl) of less than 3 micrograms and a secchi disk (sd) reading deeper than 13' means a lake is Oligotrophic; TP from 13-25 ug/l, Chl of 3-7 ug/l and a SD from 13 to 6.5' is Mesotrophic; from TP 26-99 ug/l, Chl 8-54 and SD of 6.5-1.5' is considered Eutrophic; beyond these figures, god forbid, is Hyper-eutrophic, sometimes poisonous water.

TSI ranking is principally a question of the total amount of phosphorus present, either free or fixed (taken up by rooted plants). Phosphorus (or phosphate) is an essential element in creating protoplasm - the living matter of plant and animal cells. It is widely available in nature and used extensively in manufacturing everything from firecrackers and soaps to animal feed, glass, steel and fertilizers. Because it is less available to algae than other requirements of life such as carbon and nitrogen which are abundant in the atmosphere, it limits photosynthesis or plant production in our lakes.

This amount of phosphorus in a body of water is calculated in terms of micrograms per liter of lake water (ug/l). Some lakes may have high concentrations of phosphorus yet still be clear due to several factors (almost all the phosphorus in Snail lake is taken up by rooted plants leaving little for algae). So a second rating based on chlorophyll is made.

Chlorophyll, the green pigment produced by algae, can be used as a measure of phytoplankton production and thus of the amount of phosphorus present in open water as opposed to the littoral areas where available phosphorus (ortho phosphorus) is taken up by macrophytes. Chlorophyll is a useful indicator of lake biomass but it does not deal with the issue of water "quality" directly since some algae is necessary for a recreational lake but it must be of the right variety. Thus, a third measure, this time of water transparency, is included in the ratings process.

The secchi disk is a simple circular disk painted in black and white stripes which is lowered into the water by means of a knotted rope. As the disk descends, algae make the disk harder to see. When the disk disappears, the depth is figured by means of the knots on the rope and that depth becomes the secchi disk reading for that lake. The secchi disk is nothing more than a visual means of linking invisible phosphorus with the more apparent chlorophyll.

The secchi disk is read in open water at the deepest point in the lake during summer as this is the time for maximum algal growth. It is a less technical indicator than either TP or chl ratings, but it is a reliable reflection of fertility and is often substituted for chl as a water quality index.

TSI values normally shift from year to year by as much as 10 units owing to differing weather conditions when the readings are taken during the summer. Changes of less than 10 units are not viewed as significant. Most Twin City lakes have not changed significantly since 1980. There are, however, exceptions.

Lake Wabasso in Shoreview suffered water quality degradation dropping from mesotrophic (TSI of 49 (TP) in 1980), to eutrophic (TSI of 65) by 1983. Conversely, Snail improved from a TSI of 54 in '80 to 48 in '85. In general, however, depth is destiny with already deep, clear lakes - George, Little Long, Minnewashta, Square and White Bear improving their water quality in the 80's, while shallow lakes - Cleary, Langdon, Parley and Whaletail - worsened.

10 cleanest Metro lakes:

Name	Location	Depth (m)	TSI	Year
Square	Washington Co.	20.7	35	85
Christmas	Shorewood	26.5	36	85
Little Long	Mound	23.2	40	84
Snail	Shoreview	9.1	48	85
Turtle	Shoreview	10	48-55	83
WhiteBear	White Bear Lake	25.3	48-50	84
Minnewashta	Carver Co.	21.3	49	84
Harriet	Minneapolis	25	50	84
George	Oak Grove	9.8	51	84
Big Marine	Washington Co.		52	84

10 dirtiest Metro lakes

Cleary	Prior Lake	2.0	69-76	84
Crystal	Robbinsdale	10.4	73	87
Deep	North Oaks	3.4	74	85
Centerville	Washington Co.	6	75	83
Parley	Carver Co.	6.1	75	87
Cedar	Scott Co.	4.6	78	84
Peltier	Washington Co.	5	80	83
Hydes	Carver Co.	5.5	84	85
Eagle	Carver Co.	3.9	89	85
Langdon	Mound	11.6	96	84

Man the Eutrophier

A 1969 study of Minneapolis lake quality conducted by Hickok and Assoc., concluded that all city lakes were "ecologically semi-degraded" with the natural balance of life altered to such a degree that "clean water lifeforms" were either entirely absent or reduced to a minimum.

Hickok's conclusion was arrived at by surveying bottom fauna as an index of water quality. It works like this: clean, non-polluted water is inhabited in its depths by a wide variety of biological life but only a few specimens of each type of organism. Polluted water on the other hand, has only a few different types of organism but many more specimens of each type. In other words, clean environments foster competition among species such that many are present but none dominate. Whereas, in a foul environment, only a limited number of species can exist but, since competition is absent, more members of each species are present.

Bottom fauna which are sensitive to pollution include mayfly nymphs and caddis fly worms - both staples of clean-running trout streams - and certain snails. Species which are tolerant of dirty water include scuds, sludge worms, leeches, flat worms and damsel flies. In order for a lake to be considered pollution-free by this method of analysis, the pollution sensitive creatures must comprise 50% or more of the total organisms present.

Yet in what is often considered Minneapolis' cleanest lake - Harriet - only nine bottom organisms were found and all were pollution tolerant. In only two lakes, Calhoun and Cedar, were pollution sensitive organisms present; in both cases they comprised less than 20% of species present.

If one can forget for a moment that the water one is swimming in seethes with blood worms, there is the matter of fishing. Harriet, Calhoun and Cedar were the only lakes where dissolved oxygen remained high enough throughout the year to support fish. Even then, oxygen fell in Calhoun at depths greater than 25' in March below what is thought possible to support fish. March is typically a rough month for eutrophic lakes since there is no wave action to mix atmospheric oxygen with surface waters and aquatic plants have been depleting

51

available oxygen all winter. Of course, such a situation may prove useful to resourceful ice fishermen.

From an aesthetic standpoint, all Minneapolis lakes had sufficient soluable phosphorous at the start of the growing season - .01 ppm - to spawn "abundant" algal blooms of the nuisance type. Not that this is unusual, it's been the case at least since 1947 when the first surveys were conducted. Nor has it been helped by the Park Board practice of diverting Mississippi River water (.034 ppm of P in 1956 at Itasca headwaters) to the

Runoff from 3 dozen drains will eventually alter lake character.

Minneapolis lakes chain when low water threatens to expose more beach.

Hickok recommended that the water quality of area lakes be monitored systematically and that the amount of runoff from streets be determined. They also suggested that a nutrient and hydrological balance sheet be prepared for each lake. There is no evidence that the city of Minneapolis or the Park Board instituted any of these recommendations. Ironically, however, the sad state of area waters outlined by Hickok serves as a transition to one of the few bright spots in the water quality picture: Joe Shapiro.

Professor Joseph Shapiro of the University of Minnesota Limnological Research Center (LRC) saw the Hickok report and responded. With Hans-Olaf Pfannkuch, Professor of Groundwater, Shapiro issued a 250 pp study of the Minneapolis Lakes Chain and the effects of urban drainage in 1973 and set up an annual citizen monitoring program to keep tabs on the situation. The report was to be a catalyst for his research in the field of biomanipulation (see below).

Shapiro did extensive research on the lakes drawing on work going all the way back to 1927. His summation was that "significant changes" had occurred, beginning with the draining of marsh areas in the second decade of this century and accelerating with the channelling of stormwater runoff into the lakes in the late 1920's and early 30's.

Using pollen analyses of sediment cores Shapiro estimates that before extensive urbanization, the Minneapolis Lakes chain tended toward the oligotrophic. But by 1940 all were receiving large amounts of runoff due to adjacent development of impervious surfaces - streets, roofs, sidewalks, etc. Calhoun was forced to accept runoff from an additional 650 acres of impervious surface as late as 1968.

Furthermore, he determined that the lakes faced a common enemy responsible for the reduction in water transparency, the loss of dissolved oxygen, and the shift in algal colonies toward the dreaded blue-green nuisance type: phosphorous steered into the lakes by 31 separate storm drains.

In fact, Shapiro estimated that the amount of phosphorous channelled into Lake Calhoun in just six months of 1971 amounted to 1.9 metric tons, or 3.5 times the threshold loading distinguishing a eutrophic Calhoun from an oligotrophic one.

Perhaps the worst case is Lake of the Isles. Originally a marsh which acted as a scrubber trapping suspended nutrients which would otherwise have gone into lakes Calhoun, Harriet and Cedar, Isles was extensively dredged around the turn of the century. While dredging may have reduced mosquito habitat and lent a more pleasing visual aspect to the area, it also created a shallow muddy basin positioned at a low point in the local topography.

Isles has thus become a perfect incubator of bullhead and carp, a hothouse for aquatic vegetation, a candidate for winterkill and - with nutrient runoff 17 times that necessary for eutrophic conditions - a leading target for future remedial measures.

Shapiro made numerous recommendations at the time - none of them implemented. But for the moment let us look at only one, that having to do with excessive phosphorous runoff from lawn fertilizer. Along with fallen leaves, dog droppings and grass clippings, lawn fertilizers are one of the most common and easily correctable sources of phosphorous pollution.

Shapiro conducted tests on 92 selected lawns gracing the shorelines of Lake Harriet in 1971. Every single soil sample revealed sufficient phosphorous already present to foster suitable lawn growth. The use of phosphorous-free fertilizer on those 92 lawns alone would reduce the amount of phosphorous loaded into Lake Harriet by 203 lbs. says Shapiro.

Phosphorous drew flak from the next area-wide water quality study, one conducted by the Metropolitan Council and released in July, 1981. The Met Council study not only found a direct correlation between too much phosphorous and reduced water transparency, but it also suggested that all 60 metro lakes investigated had enough P stored in bottom sediments to affect their water clarity for years to come even without new loadings.

Lake Restoration

Lake restoration techniques can affect the lake fundamentally, altering ecosystem interrelations, or cosmetically, treating the symptoms of eutrophication. The most direct of course, is simply not letting phosphorus get to the lake in the first place.

Diversion is also the best long-term solution to excessive nutrient inflow. Unfortunately, it is both difficult and expensive in urban watersheds.

Nutrients can enter the lake from point or non-point sources. Control of point sources involves treating discharges from industrial locations and domestic sewage systems. Raw sewage commonly contains 1-20 mg/l of P, making it extremely eutrophic (26-99 ppb P). Secondary treatment reduces P to a level of .1-2 ppm. Tertiary treatment at a modern treatment plant removes P leaving 0.03-.6 ppm, or water "dirtier" than the

Mississippi River as it passes through Minneapolis. Collection and treatment of domestic sewage and industrial wastes is an obvious necessity from the standpoint of recreational water quality. Increasingly, diversion of non-point sources - stormwater runoff from streets, roofs, parking lots and other impervious surfaces - is seen as a means of improving a lake's long-term trophic status. This usually involves a comprehensive municipal effort to separate sanitary sewage systems (domestic sewage) from stormwater collection. The Twin Cities are a national leader in adopting a separate collection system so that in time of heavy rains, stormwater funnelled into the Mississippi River never comes in contact with sewage. Of only 15 such systems built world-wide, 9 resulted in significant improvements in lake ecology.

This is good news to river users downstream but it wasn't meant to clean up the Mississippi, only to cut fecal colony reproduction to the point no one got sick. In truth, stormwater runoff is a flood of contamination.

Those sources of P too numerous to elaborate - the "non-points" - are you and me and the leaves of the oak and pollen of the willow, cigarettes, oil, animal droppings and $.40 styrofoam cups. Construction activity adds heavily to the degradation of urban lakes and their stunned, reeling watersheds. One can witness this at numerous points along the distressed Minneapolis Chain of Lakes as outlet pipes run a sour apple green after summer downpours.

A single solution such as diversion of runoff would be expensive (though very effective). More frequent street sweeping, firmer controls on the disposal of yard litter and kitty's litter, better recycling of oil and paints, earlier plowing and less salt - plus secondary treatment: filtration, screening, aeration before street wastes entered the lakes - would help significantly.

Efforts to restore a lake, or trying to resuscitate a previous balance of ecological forces, "seldom succeed" according to the Met Council. Naturally, all fall short of diversion in effectiveness.

Dredging is the most commonly used technique to deal with the problem of sediments filling navigation channels and pumping P into the water. It's ill effects are as temporary as its beneficial results judging from most studies, but it's a quick solution and one acceptable in areas where a lake's pristine character is not at issue.

Harvesting of offending weeds and other biomass helps clear the water of P producers but most is still hanging about in the water or hiding in the lake bottom. It might make marginal improvements in water clarity in already transparent waters, but it couldn't turn around a lake clouded with eutrophying nutrients.

Nor do chemical treatments with copper sulfate, an algicide, work for long since the dying algae release P for future uptake. Herbicides such as Paraquat and 2,4-D kill nuisance weeds, such as Eurasian milfoil but, again, phosphorus escapes for take- up elsewhere.

Pinning hopes on exotic solutions (see below - Biomanipulation) is unrealistic given a badly tilted environment. Diversion and treatment remain the best hope for clean water in the future.

Biomanipulation:
An Ecosystem Approach to Lake Restoration

One of the more visible - and annoying - consequences of lake aging from a human perspective is the algal coating that takes over the surface area of eutrophic lakes as they fill-in and warm. Algae are really simple plants sometimes consisting of a single cell. Almost all lakes - even the cleanest - harbor some type of algae. Algae, or phytoplankton, are part of the 'crop' grown by aquatic environments.

But some algae - blue-green filamentous algae - signal the decline of desirable lake inhabitants and indicate a lake ecosystem out of balance. Blue-green algae explosions indicate nutrient overloading and a dangerously eutrophic system. Unfortunately, blue-greens have taken over many of our area lakes.

Dr. Joe Shapiro of the University of Minnesota thinks he may have a cure. Typically, the shift from benign forms of algae to the blue-greens which force out others, is thought to depend on the amount of phosphorus (P) allowed to run off lawns and streets into the lake. Sources of P are ubiquitous; not only lawn fertilizer but leaves, grass clippings, seed cases and even dust.

Preventing these numerous non-point sources from getting into our lakes would be a very expensive proposition indeed. But Shapiro believes there is a better way. He calls it biomanipulation.

Shapiro's studies of highly eutrophic lakes led him to believe that aquatic relationships were more complex than was indicated by drawing a direct correlation between the fact that more phosphorus runoff = more algae. He noted that eutrophic lakes often had very large populations of carp and bullheads, bottom feeding fish that excrete phosphorus and ammonia (a nitrogen-hydrogen compound used to make fertilizers): enough P (as much as half the P found in a lake can be traced to carp) and ammonia he discovered, to raise water pH stimulating huge blue-green algal blooms.

He also saw that large gamefish - predators such as walleye and pike - were relatively few in number, at least not sufficient to keep down the populations of stunted perch and sunfish that apparently take over eutrophic waters. Shapiro observed that these three characteristics were evident in almost all eutrophic lakes: bottom feeders, stunted sunfish and perch, and blue-green algal blooms.

Yet, when these eutrophic lakes filled in to the point where there was insufficient oxygen to supply fish over the winter ("winterkill") the lake would suddenly become quite clear. As an example, there is the case of Wirth Lake in Minneapolis. Normally, a highly eutrophic environment with lots of algae and a water transparency of 0.7 - 1.6 m. in July, Wirth became extremely clear - 4.5 m. - in the spring of 1978 after a rotenone treatment killed off most of its fish.

Shapiro noticed something else taking place in Lake Harriet, Minneapolis' cleanest lake. While technically eutrophic, with its water draining from Calhoun and Cedar lakes, and a similar amount of lawn and street runoff, Harriet remained much cleaner. Shapiro, a biologist, asked himself: could it be that something in the aquatic community besides phosphorus was the deciding factor in water clarity?

Shapiro set up a series of experiments in a small Twin Cities lake. Using nets he created various enclosures in the lake where he could control amounts of phosphorus, bottom feeders, perch, algae and zooplankton. Within days the experiment had yielded amazing results.

Those pens containing bottom feeders or perch were thick with blue-green algae,but those with no fish were clear and yet the amount of phosphorus was consistent throughout the lake. Shapiro ran a fine mesh through the clean water and discovered teeming colonies of Daphnia pulex, a large (2mm) zooplankton crustacean known to graze on green algae.

Repeated testing and trips to Lake Harriet confirmed his findings: in lakes where small perch and sunfish eat most of the Daphnia, or bottom feeders pollute the waters with ammonia thus killing the zooplankton, algal populations shift from green to the blue-green variety and the lake becomes messy and undesirable.

Yet in lakes such as Harriet where there is a balance between large fish and their prey, and rough fish are kept in check, Daphnia exist in large numbers grazing back the algae and keeping the water clear.

Biomanipultion was tried in St. Paul's Como Lake in 1985 with results remarkably true to Shapiro's predictions. First, rotenone was used to kill the existing population of rough fish and stunted bluegill sunfish. In a few months, large Daphnia appeared and began to graze down algae. Soon the phosphorus content of the lake dropped and water clarity improved. However, DNR workers restocked Como with bluegills which promptly ate the Daphnia allowing phosphorus levels to rise with a corresponding decrease in lake transparency.

Shapiro has since refined his research concluding that the different levels of lake biota are so interdependent that, as one level becomes more abundant, the level below necessarily decreases and vice-versa. He has proved that pesticide runoff from mosquito control spraying is extremely toxic to Daphnia and thus detrimental to water clarity. And he's demonstrated that circulating lake water helps control rapid increases in pH as a result of rough fish population increases. He now hopes to convince policy makers that eutrophication can be stopped, even reversed, through biomanipulation — cheaper and more effective than eliminating all non-point sources of phosphorus.

Shapiro's lessons should be of importance to anyone who has noticed that Lake of the Isles (clean after a 1976 winterkill) is again thick with carp and Lake Calhoun is infested with swarms of 2-3" perch.

Chapter 3

Central Lakes

Fish Finders:
From U-boats to Your Boat

Imagine the crew of 'Das Boot' calmly aiming their torpedoes at a fat merchant ship in the North Atlantic circa 1943. Suddenly, half the British Navy is bearing down on the hapless U-boat, hurling tons of deadly depth charges as they attack.

The incredible efficiency of Allied destroyers must have come as a cruel shock to the Wermacht. At first they suspected treason, but it finally dawned on them that their devastating losses were the result of superior British and U.S. technology: sonar (sound navigation ranging). Modern depth sounders give today's angler a similar advantage over his quarry, but unless you want Kurt and his cronies to escape, you had better know how to use it. The first step is the machinery itself.

Depth sounder technology grew out of radio wave (radar) experiments conducted by the British in the 1920's. Sonar simply substituted sound, or pressure waves, for radio, or electromagnetic waves, in order to detect objects by means of their reflected wave lengths.

Ocean sonar can be directed through several miles of water with lethal impact on schools of tuna, halibut and mackerel as well as submarines. Inland lake depth sounding as currently practiced in the sport fishing industry hasn't taken such a mouthful yet and confines itself to interpreting echoes from a narrow beam, or cone, directly under the boat. Yet the latest 'fish finding' implements have undergone a rapid evolution since hitting the consumer market, metamorphisizing into light-weight, efficient, portable and cheap kiss-n-tell biographies of any species in the vicinity.

All depth sounders operate via a transducer, a ceramic crystal which converts electrical energy from a battery into an acoustic impulse. This impulse is then projected through the water at 4,945 feet per second. When the impulse encounters a solid object, a portion is reflected back to the transducer which reconverts the signal to electrical energy. Since the distance sound travels in a given medium (in this case, water) is known (4,945 feet per second), the returning echo is timed and divided by 2 (the journey out and back) to produce a measurement of distance.

Depth sounders generally use either a high (200 kilohertz) or a low (50 kilohertz) frequency depending on the particular task. Either frequency is still higher than that of the fishes' hearing range so there is no question of alarming *les poissons.*

Low frequency sound waves are used to penetrate deep water but they have a longer pulse length and therefore poorer resolution, or fish separation. Most inland fishermen require measurements of hundreds of feet rather than thousands so they can utilize the higher frequency band which offers shorter pulse lengths and better resolution.

In terms of sequence of appearance, the first machines to arrive on the market were the chart recorders which drew a picture of the bottom and intervening objects by means of a stylus and a paper scroll. Charts offered excellent resolution of detail but had several drawbacks. They were expensive to operate requiring reams of paper; they drew a great deal of power and thus needed a large battery; they didn't work well at high speeds and weren't very portable. On the other hand, they provided a permanent record of bottom contour and outlined fish in easily recognizable markings.

Next came the LEDs, or Light Emitting Diodes, used in the flasher-type locators. These machines give an accurate reading of depth and bottom strata at 60 mph and are quite portable. However, flashers depict fish in an indirect way, requiring practice in order to discern the presence of finned inhabitants by thickness of the returning signal. Also, the flasher cannot discriminate between fish and weeds when the boat is moving.

Many anglers combine the chart and the flasher in simultaneous operation, using the flasher to spot fish or contour, and the chart to provide a permanent, easy to interpret, pictorial display. But before one could say, 'Do you take Visa?', along comes the LCDs (Liquid Crystal Display) which was designed to supplant both the chart and the LED.

The LCDs (or LCRs: Liquid Crystal Recorders) are actually a compromise offering a momentary record (without the need for a supply of paper) and a whole series of graphic fish alarms. They also work at considerably less power eliminating the need for a heavy 12-volt battery, are easier to read in bright sunlight than the flasher and take up less space than a panfish fillet. But, as befits a compromise, LCDs are seen by many as lacking the quality of the more specialized product, i.e., among other problems, they are more difficult to read than the paper graph under certain light conditions.

The chief problem is in the image resolution. LCDs display in pixels, or picture dots similar to those which bear the image in newspapers, magazines and other printed matter. The more pixels, the sharper the image. Since each pixel in an LCD is literally filled with liquid, getting more pixels on the screen is a pretty heady job even in an era of miniaturization.

Where a good chart recorder may have as many as 1 million pixels to the square inch, a small LCD may have only 120 vertical pixels. Thus, in 120 feet of water, each pixel represents 1 foot in the water column — a fish must be very large and in the center of the cone to be visible.

There is also the complication caused by manufacturers who rate their machines differently, some using total number of pixels on screen, others the number on the vertical axis, still others offer the number per square inch. Undoubtedly, some of this confusion will be alleviated by newer models offering more pixels and better ratings, but perspective buyers should be aware of other problems as well.

A difficulty with the earlier LCDs is the fact that unlike a flasher, they do not reveal the mysteries of bottom composition. This is an esoteric but essential part of fish lore as bottom composition says a great deal about fish location. Smart fishermen will not be without this feature since an ordinary LCD may show where fish are but will not tell you (as bottom strata will) what they are dining upon.

Early LCDs did not have the capacity to discriminate between soft bottoms of sand or mud vs. rock except by watching the screen for signs of increased power output signalling a return from soft strata. Such information was not easily come by for the casual observer. Current LCD technology should feature Gray Line discrimination whereby band width on the screen will vary according to bottom hardness much like a flasher unit.

LCDs must quickly solve such problems in the face of competition from CRTs. The CRT uses a Cathode Ray Tube much like a television set to deliver a high-quality image in living color. Resolution is excellent since the image is made up of super-tiny electronic dots. Up-to-date CRT technology is expensive ($1,000) if you want the 18-color screens available. However, a simple two-tone system, orange on gray like many computer monitors, can be had for around $200.

The CRT uses a computer program to assign colors according to the strength of a returning signal. Also, large fish appear as arcs on the screen (difficult with the square pixels of the LCD). Both means of display — color density and arcs — assist in differentiating fish right down to telling a lake trout from a salmon at 20 fathoms.

CRTs can be equipped with a VHS cassette to provide a permanent record like the chart recorder. CRTs are fast becoming a favorite of Great Lake captains (sufficient resolution to trace down-riggers) and professional fishermen. But wait, we haven't mentioned loran!

Loran (long range navigation) is a system which operates like a depth sounder over land. Again, acoustic pulses of standard length are sent out, this time to known surface positions, and the response interval measured to determine exact longitude and latitude. Given the proper co-ordinates, loran gives your vessel the capacity of locating a silver dollar in mid-Atlantic (well, almost).

Costing anywhere from $1,500 to $3,000, loran can do many wondrous things: in addition to present location, loran can save numerous way points (sets of co-ordinates) in memory and serve them up on an "electronic canvas" plotting the actual path to a designated spot complete with magnetic bearing, distance, and estimated time of arrival. Built-in guides show off-course errors and steering corrections.

The very latest technology couples loran, fish finding and depth sounding to provide species identification in shallow (high frequency) or deep water (low frequency), and will even display in yards the signal area under the boat from which the screen readings are taken, ending forever the confusion resulting from readings at the edge of the signal beam and its center.

How To Use Modern Electronics

Nowadays, every fishing magazine boasts a "scientific" approach to angling (if not to prose), with the result that information that used to be locked up in the tight smiles of the old-timers with 25 years on the lake, is now available to anyone willing to throw on a little Muskol. Scientific certainly describes the search for stream trout, a sport which owes as much to hydrology, limnology and entomology as it does to mythology.

A stream, of course, lends itself more easily to observation and analysis than does a large lake. But the principle having been established, it didn't take long for Dr. Science to arrive at Your Lake.

Still, though electronics might tell you depth, water temperature, pH, clarity and even sound an alarm when a fish is spotted, they don't put fish in the boat. To paraphrase an old cliche, you can lead a fisherman to water but you can't make him think. Just ask John Daily, fisheries biologist, head of the DNR's Hatchery operations and an avid fisherman whose own use of electronics has increased his effectiveness "30%."

"Give the average fisherman the whole array of gadgets and even tell him how to use them, but they won't master the presentation, so it's all for nothing," says Daily.

Daily claims new techniques are lost on most anglers who lose confidence in new information before they've mastered it. "The fisherman who doesn't understand what they've been told will waste their time on low percentage efforts and, when these fail, will revert back to their old habits, they have confidence in those."

Granted, Daily's information-gathering ritual before setting forth on strange waters is daunting: in addition to topo maps, info on forage fish, alkalinity, substratum, weed types, etc., Daily spends two hours touring the lake while watching his depth-finder before even wetting a line. Daily's techniques are those of a professional but they can be abbreviated somewhat for those who favor a more casual outing. But there simply is no way to short-cut the obligation to utilize - correctly - the knowledge coming from your depth-sounder.

"A depth-sounder's job is to find the optimal habitat, or structure," says Charles Anderson, DNR research scientist. "Next to knowing seasonal patterns, structure is the most important thing in finding fish."

The primacy of structure is universal. Structure is basically any change in lake bottom conditions which attract and hold fish. There are numerous bottom conditions - rock piles, points, reefs, sand bars, etc. - which, once known and understood, will yield similar results. This is the reason old hands on a particular lake always catch most of the fish. "It's the old folk wisdom we've all heard," recites Anderson, "10% of the fishermen catch 90% of the fish."

Just ask Roland Martin, a household name in piscatorial pro-fishency, how he employs his electronics: "I use my sounder to locate sloping mid-lake points which extend some distance from shore because they are the easiest to fish, offering shallow feeding grounds, deep-water cover and a continuous mix of air and water. The contrast in depths offers temperature changes and nutrient up-welling, and where there's nutrients, there's plankton and small fish. And nearby, of course, large fish."

Martin pays close attention to water temperature as well. "Water temperature alone eliminates 90% of the possible patterns I might use," says Martin. For instance, after spawning in the spring as water temperature warms to about 45 degrees, walleyes will seek water temperatures between 52 and 66 degrees for the remainder of the summer with 58 degrees preferred.

Each fish species has its own range of preferred temperatures and these are important to keep in mind. Remember that fish are cold-blooded creatures and respond physiologically to extremes in their temperature environment. Fish outside their specialized niches are apt to be propelled there by reasons other than hunger and thus they may be difficult or impossible to catch.

Light-sensitive walleyes may be in shallow water not to feed but to re-oxygenate their bodies in surface waters where air is absorbed from the atmosphere into the lake; a northern pike may be resting in very cold water in order to bring their body temperatures down after an energetic chase at a lesser depth.

When fish are found where they should be, that is in the vicinity of their favorite seasonal restaurant, it's reasonable to assume they will be more active in pursuit of a meal.

Now, how does this information tie in with *presentation* to produce fish? First of all, there is the season to consider. This fact is crucial to walleye location and is akin to temperature. After spawning, large females will join the smaller males in shallow bays in water generally 8-10 feet deep. They will likely seek structure of sand or gravel near muck or mud bottom.

At other times, walleyes would not be found near soft bottom but this is spring and walleyes feed predominantly on abundant insect hatches at this time of year and that means mud. If you find fish on your depth sounder offer them a slip-bobber and minnow combination at appropriate depth, or a Lindy 1/8 ounce Fuzz-E-Grub jigged slowly and near bottom to imitate the surface-rising flight of the mayfly nymph.

Yellow, chartreuse or orange jigs work well in dark waters; purple or black in clear water (visibility over 3 feet as rated on a Secchi disk - do you want to catch fish or not?).

If you are fishing a shallow lake which has warmed up to 52-55 degrees, you may go to a larger 1/4-3/8 ounce jig. The newer, stronger monofilament lines let you get by with as little as 4# test although 6# is more typical.

Trolling offshore in shallow water is often effective in early spring (and late fall). Use the depth-finder to locate shoreline breaks (drop-offs) and the outside edge of weedlines where large predator fish gather to stage their forays after smaller prey.

Troll live bait over weed tops using an open bail and a slip-sinker rig at a depth of 4 feet or so. Hold the line loosely in your fingers until you feel tension (graphite rods of about 7 feet are excellent for this), let go of the line for 3-5 seconds, then reel in the slack and set the hook.

Artificial lures, either Rapalas or other crank baits, can be trolled much the same way (close the bail) along the deep-water side of bars or over the top of reefs. They are also quite potent fished from shore if you don't have a boat. Choose low-light conditions just before sunrise or after sundown to cast near inlets and narrows, or off points.

Casting or trolling with live-bait and plugs are excellent techniques if the water is relatively warm and fish are dispersed and actively feeding as they often are in low-light. However, Opener is often conducted under nearly opposite conditions, with fish sluggish and bunched near bottom, the sun bright but water cold. These circumstances favor slip-bobbers and Lindy rigs of precise length to insure the bait wriggles immediately before the walleyes' appetite.

Slip-bobbers are quite popular because they can be cast to the spot indicated by bottom structure without the necessity of placing the boat directly over the fish where it may spook them. Experienced fishermen position the boat to allow wave movement to drift the bobber and bait over the fish. To repeat, use your fish-finding device to locate promising structure or to find the fish themselves before anchoring some slight distance away.

If there is too much wave action to keep the bobber on top of the fish, switch to a Lindy slip-sinker rig but do so thoughtfully. Keep in mind that bright light will keep fish near bottom but significant wave action refracts or breaks up light so fish are less affected by clear skies. Since fish may be suspended anywhere from 2-10 feet off the bottom, you must adjust the length of the leader accordingly.

A short leader (less than 3 feet) is indicated if: a) water is colder than species preference; b) water is stained or highly colored; c) a cold front is the major local weather pattern; or d) fish are on bottom. Use a long leader (3-10 feet), a floating jig head and/or inflated night crawler if: a) fish are suspended off bottom; b) water clarity is generally good; and c) water is warm.

In the former case, a short leader gives the fisherman better "feel" of the situation when fish are likely to be biting tentatively. You want to be able to set the hook quickly without having to take up a lot of slack in the leader once you feel it's taken the bait. A long leader on the other hand, allows aggressive fish to grab the bait and swim freely with it without detecting the fisherman and spitting the hook.

In deep lakes which stratify during summer months, the thermocline, or region where temperature changes rapidly as warm surface water gives way to cold water from the deep profundal zone, is a key to fish location. This area acts like "structure" in that it is a likely holding depth for cold-water predator species. Here, higher surface oxygen concentrations mingle with nutrients pushed upward by gaseous releases from the decomposition of bottom sediments.

The result is a rich current of life as surface oxygen mixes with bottom elements such as phosphorous and nitrogen. This chemical stew is then absorbed by light-sensitive phytoplankton (single-celled plant life) which in turn are grazed by tiny animals (zooplankton) who are then consumed by baitfish - alewives, shad, etc. - which subsequently become a banquet for gamefish like walleye and trout.

The thermocline rises and falls throughout the lake de-pending on the season, but is most pronounced - and useful - during summer when fish retreat to its safety and resources. A fish-finder can locate the thermocline generally by finding concentrations of baitfish. The addition of a pH meter and temperature gauge will make certain. On large deep lakes like Saganaga, baits are attached to downrigger balls much like in the Great Lakes of Superior and Michigan.

Another novel technique that can be coordinated with a depth finder is reported by Dick Sternberg of the Hunting and Fishing Library. Named Griz-jigging after its inventor, Dick Grzywinski, it involves fast trolling along the edges of sandbars.

The idea is to locate fish holding near the bar and begin a horizontal jigging pattern. Run the boat parallel the fish and let out line at about 4-5 times the depth at which they're holding.

Employing a stiff 7' rod, "snap" the rod tip forward quickly about 3' using only the wrist. Immediately return the rod tip to the starting position allowing the jig to settle back on a slack line. When the line tenses, repeat the process.

Frequent snaps will hook walleyes who inhale the jig as it falls. A 1/8-1/4 oz. Northland Fireball jig with a trailer hook completes the ensemble.

As summer arrives and the water warms, action focuses on reefs around 15-18' deep utilizing leeches and night crawlers. Whether fast trolling a crankbait or using a slip-sinker under big water, windy conditions, add sufficient weight (up to 1 oz.) 3' ahead of bait to keep your offering deep.

A few springtime hints: tie a piece of hot pink or yellow yarn on your hook in front of live bait to attract attention; if fishing at night, use a lighted bobber or floating plug with irregular retrieve; and, if fishing in early morning or at dusk, cast ahead of your boat into very shallow water (2') instead of trolling behind. Good luck.

Reinvest in Minnesota: Parity Begins at Home

The scene: two hunters are returning the quarter mile to their car. They've fallen into waist-deep water coming out of a slough and are slowly freezing. A deer presented itself for an easy shot but neither could shoot because they couldn't get their heavy mittens off in time. When they arrive at the car, they can't find the keys. They hold a brief dialogue: "Can you imagine this mess? Give me one good reason we shouldn't move to Florida." "Because," comes the answer, "we're having too much fun."

Minnesota is simply too much fun — it's the only legitimate excuse for living here. This conclusion was pretty much taken for granted until 1984 when a very unfunny thing happened. A Commission appointed by then Gov. Rudy Perpich to find new methods of capitalizing on the state's quality of outdoor life discovered a wormy apple: Minnesota sportsmen were leaving the state!

That's right. Native dollars had suddenly taken flight, becoming the single largest source of outstate tourist and license money in almost every state and Canadian province bordering Minnesota.

The Commission to Promote Hunting and Fishing, composed of outdoor enthusiasts, conservationists and legislators, was now forced to face criticisms coming from the $1.5 billion hunting and fishing industry: how come the fish are getting smaller, pheasants and waterfowl tougher to find? The answer had a lot to do with those vanishing sports dollars.

Simply put, Minnesota was less and less fun. Since 1950, five million acres of natural habitat had been destroyed through commercial and agricultural development; 85% of the state's wetlands were lost and 99.9% of its native prairies had gone the way of the buffalo.

The dilemma can be phrased simply: an increasing population which places more emphasis on outdoor recreation finds itself in an environment where wildlife suffers from an ever decreasing natural habitat.

Meanwhile, the Division of Fish and Wildlife of the DNR saw their budget - 90% of which is paid for by sportsmen - remain static. Managing the status quo takes most of that budget, leaving only 8% ($2.4 million in 1988) to be spent on habitat acquisition and improvement.

"Hunters and fishermen are paying their way," says Ray Norrgard, RIM Coordinator for the DNR, "but everyone benefits anytime we can improve water quality, reduce non-point pollution or practice sound land management.

"We had to find a way to go beyond hunting and fishing fees as a stable funding source for the environment. We needed to tap the rest of society who benefit from wise use of natural resources."

The answer, from the Commission's point of view, was the Reinvest in Minnesota (RIM) program. The program bears some explanation because it is complex, rife with regulation and eminently democratic.

As conceived by the state legislature, RIM would sell $60 million worth of bonds over a 6-yr. period with proceeds divided between the Minnesota Department of Agriculture and the DNR. The Agriculture Department would run a land-bank where farmers would be paid to take marginal land out of production by way of 10-yr. or permanent easements.

Politically, the farm economy would receive some assistance and land which could raise more pheasants than soybeans could go back into the 'natural' column. The Agriculture Department side of RIM would be aimed at the 10% of Minnesota's 23 million agricultural acres which are either seasonally flooded or too steep for optimal yield.

Local Soil and Water Conservation Districts set the Agriculture agenda, reviewing applications for the RIM reserve acreage and determining priorities according to local experience and conditions.

For example, in the southwest part of the state, with a very high degree of land cultivation and few free-standing wood lots, potential deer wintering habitat would likely be selected. Whereas, in the southeast, with its deep valleys and sink-holes, land-banking would be targeted toward erosion control and ground-water clean-up.

Under RIM, the state DNR has multiple obligations. One aim of the RIM measure is the aspen program. Aspen is a fast-growing tree which has recently become valuable for its use in the paper and construction industries. Before its rise in popularity however, aspen was overlooked and this caused many aspen stands to over-mature.

The DNR will spend several million dollars over the life of RIM to log-off unusable stands so the state economy can produce more of the saleable softwood. Clear-cutting over-mature aspen - while not one of your more attractive sights - provides open areas where the fast growing aspen saplings can be used as cover for grouse and song birds, edible browse for deer and moose.

Another objective is prairie restoration. In 1989, the DNR spent $300,000 to burn 9,000 acres at 160 sites. The controlled burnings assist native grasses such as bluestem and Indian grass, says Norrgard, because these grasses perpetuate themselves under a 'regime of fire.'

That is, spring fires retard the growth of imported plants such as brome and bluegrass which are 'cool-season,' growing and maturing in spring or early summer. The natives are 'warm-season,' therefore, early burning reduces plant litter to nutrient-rich ash and allows sunlight to warm the soil setting the stage for natives to seed in late summer.

Burning also prevents woody species such as willow from taking over the prairie. Thanks to RIM, the process of restoring prairies can proceed at triple its previous pace.

In fact, "enhancement" of the environment is a critical ingredient on the RIM menu. Projects which have languished for years on the DNR wish-list due to lack of necessary personnel, equipment or funds, can be resurrected and implemented.

Three projects about to be undertaken by the DNR demonstrate the scope of rehabilitation possible thanks to RIM:

1) $40,000 for improving a mile of West Indian Creek in Wabasha County. The improvements include placing rock riprap to control erosion, create fish cover under stream banks and in deep pools, and provide a clean gravel bottom — the riffles conducive to breeding aquatic insects. These steps should lead to an environment suitable for natural trout reproduction. Not only will this mean less reliance on put-n-take hatchery stocking, but it also addresses past land use problems dating back to the 1870's.

2) $72,000 to assist a small lake in Scott County, Carl's Lake, become a year-around sport fishing resource. An aeration system has been installed (one of five made possible through RIM) to prevent winter-kill and a dike constructed adjacent the lake for a northern pike spawning area.

3) $69,000 for major shoreline reconstruction on Lake Winnebigoshish which will not only prevent erosion from silting up shallow lake areas, but will also provide loose gravel for walleye spawning.

For those who hunt, here's a sample of RIM stocking-stuffers:

1) $480,000 for work with private forest landowners in the northeast to improve forest cover for two species, ruffed grouse and white-tail deer.

2) Purchase easements on 1,500 acres of alternative 'food pastures' for the state's burgeoning goose population. RIM funds will be spent to set up small 1-2 acres plots next to wetlands to intercept young geese before they hit private cropland where their Giant Canadian appetites can decimate early growth soybean and corn fields.

Most spectacular of all RIM missions however, is CHPS: the Critical Habitat Private Sector matching program. This RIM offspring earmarks funds to acquire lands primarily home to endangered species.

The unusual part of this initiative is that as a matching fund, CHPS donors dictate the agenda putting up half the cost of areas they want protected. In two years, the DNR has matched $2 million in private giving.

Working with private donors, the DNR has acquired two areas of particular beauty and fragility, the A Shau Valley and

Blackhoof Wildlife Management Areas (WMA). In the A Shau near Kimball, deer and wild turkey romp and multiply on a string of wooded hills rising out of a large marsh nurtured by the annual flooding of the Clearwater River. The Blackhoof is even more impressive.

Off for a morning of fishing in the valley of the Blackhoof.

The Blackhoof WMA takes its name from the Blackhoof River, a serpentine arrangement of pools and riffles eating its way through the clay sediments which once made up the bottom of huge glacial Lake Nemadji. Some 12,000 years ago Lake Nemadji rose 450' above the current level of Lake Superior. Today, the old lake basin has been drained leaving a hazy blue smudge on the eastern horizon to motorists hurtling by on the Interstate some 50 miles south of Duluth.

Within the basin is a pre-historic environment virtually untouched by the hand of man. Plateaus of pine and birch suddenly slump away into steep 100' gorges ruled by truculent alder and mammoth, six-foot ferns. Dimly lit ravines are commonplace landscape features as rivulets become creeks, creeks turn into streams and streams swell into rivers.

Each drop of rain which falls in the vicinity is dragged to the valley floor, scratching the thin forest soils and bleeding red clay into the Nemadji River.

74

It's a moist, bewildering, twilight world of aspen, birch and maple on south-facing slopes, spruce and balsam on the north. The area is excellent deer wintering habitat and is known for its populations of woodcock and grouse.

The Blackhoof itself is the finest river in the watershed and boasts 10 miles of prime brook and brown trout water; a run of steelhead come up the Nemadji from Lake Superior each spring.

Thanks to a grant of 1,600 acres from the Nature Conservancy, DNR control of this pristine habitat can stifle incompatible development. Currently, the Blackhoof WMA is wooded and inaccessible and plans are for it to stay that way with only a minimum of roads and bridges on the drawing table. For the foreseeable future it will be paradise without a parking lot.

With the passage of the Environmental Trust Fund Amendment, RIM monies are stable and guaranteed, no longer subject to annual budget vagaries. All in all, something good is happening to the environment and those who love the land and the "fun" of life in Minnesota can look forward to many years of happy "*rim*iniscence."

Special Regulations
May Become the Norm

Last year Minnesotans bought 2.3 million fishing licenses. That's a million more anglers than the entire population of the state - men, women and pee wee hockey players - in 1950, only 41 years ago. And these new piscivorous predators don't come to the shores of the lake with thick braided dacron, a weight tied to a rope for a 'fish locator' and steel rods that wouldn't bend in a typhoon.

The effect of increased angling pressure and improved angling technique can be quantified if proper historical records can be found. DNR Fisheries research biologists Donald Olson and Paul Cunningham did just that analyzing 38 years of catches in 120 lakes (62,000 acres) in an area of northwestern Minnesota. The fish were submitted to an annual contest sponsored by Fuller's Tackle, Park Rapids.

All 114,000 fish were tallied and the results show trophy-sized fish steadily declining for all species: Large muskies disappeared by 1940; northern pike peaked in '48 (mean wt. of pike dropped from 10.1 pounds in the 1930's, to 6.8 pounds in the 80's); walleyes have declined in size since '72; and large-mouth bass since '79. Even large black crappies and blue gills (2 pounds) have nearly disappeared. Ponder from a moment that when these larger fish were available, daily limits for walleye and largemouth were 15; northern 25.

A similar situation developed on massive walleye fishery Lake Winnibigoshish. There, fishing pressure increased 771% between the 1930's and 70's with the result, according to a DNR planning team, that "walleye yields increased, while age and size of fish caught has declined."

Thinking differs on whether fish can grow as smart as the fisherman. As reported in the In-Fisherman, a 4-year study of an Illinois' lake which allowed only catch-n-release showed that all fish over 1' in length were caught.

"Some bass can be caught and re-caught on the same lure," says DNR hatchery supervisor, John Daily. "Still others don't seem susceptible to angling pressure; they get educated very quickly." Daily says some large bass, those over five years old, are either difficult or impossible to catch. "They're loners, they can be caught, but it isn't enough just to find them, though that too can be difficult. It would take an expert angler, skilled in presentation."

Al Lindner once received special permission to attempt to catch, tag and release every fish he could in a small lake near Brainerd to demonstrate the effectiveness of the new technology - or the survival skills of the fish. Even when the guru of 'scientific' angling tried, he couldn't catch them all.

But, according to Paul Wingate, DNR research manager, even educated fish "lack the ability to pass this knowledge on to their offspring." Likewise, even though it may not be possible to deplete a lake of all it's large predators, the lake's species balance, it's genetic potential and even its water clarity could be affected by the removal of the lake's 'keystone' predator.

This dominant predator maintains balance in the aquatic community by preying heavily on forage fish and keeping less desirable species in check. If some of the undesirables, such as carp or bullheads, were allowed to reproduce without predation, the result would be more bottom-feeders and, eventually, a warmer, muddier lake. Clearly, there is a lot at stake.

Wingate says studies have shown that the angler of 30 years ago only fished "effectively" for 1 1/2 hours per outing; the current angler is twice as effective per hour spent on the water.

Nor is greater hatchery output the answer, claims Wingate. "In lakes like those of the southwest with little or no natural reproduction and heavy angling pressure, it's the only way to provide a satisfactory fishing experience. But in lakes with natural reproduction, stocked fish only displace existing fish, weakening the genetic strain."

There are 5,000 lakes in Minnesota the DNR considers "fish" lakes. Certainly, improved habitat can help create improved fishing, but other changes will have to be made as well. One avenue is increased utilization of catch-n-release.

Recent work indicates catch-n-release can greatly reduce fish mortality, says DNR research scientist Charles Anderson. "The key is where the fish is hooked (gills or stomach are fatal) and prompt release; 95% of walleyes will survive proper handling." Not all agree.

Some claim that anglers are using catch-n-release - so called - to fish longer, substituting larger fish recently caught with "release" of smaller fish on the stringer for hours. This "stringer sorting" is hardly the intent of catch-n-release (it's also against the law) since those stringer fish are in all probability, doomed.

Others contend that there are more variables involved than simply releasing a healthy-looking fish. Fish pulled from deep, cool water through hot surface water after a struggle that builds toxic gases in their blood, do not have a good chance for survival. They also insist that even a 20% mortality figure means a doubling of the legal limit if an angler catches 15 and releases 12, three of which are unlikely to survive.

Regardless of which figures you believe, any attempt at catch-n-release would be assisted by these precautions: remove all but the last, or trailing set of trebles, or switch to single hooks on spinning and trolling lures; bend down the barbs on all hooks; keep fish intended for release in the water if possible; and use a glove to open the mouth of toothy specimens rather than gaffing and hoisting them into the boat.

Another route of equal importance to fish resource management are those rules falling under the broad aegis of Special Regulations.

Regulation, of course, began with bag limits in 1891 followed by sport fishing licensing in 1927. By "special regs," we mean the enhancement of the fishery. Daily explains: "This way we can develop more specialized environments requiring differing levels of angling expertise. Some people may want to catch a limit of smaller fish for the table; others want to challenge themselves, maybe take only one large fish or keep none at all."

"Special regs," says Wingate, "allow us to tailor an approach for individual lakes. Say the species in a particular lake are being beat upon, we can alter existing fishing patterns to produce a quality experience."

As his example, Wingate chose Mille Lacs, celebrated Superbowl of walleye production. Thanks to over-fishing, walleyes, though numerous, were averaging smaller weights. Now check your 1991 Fishing Regulations under "Experimental Waters." Notice night fishing is closed during the spring spawning run and only one fish over 20 inches can be taken per day. Such regulation is designed to boost the numbers of large fish. Wingate claims it's working - "the average walleye harvested has grown from 15 inches to 18 inches."

This stringer looks and tastes delicious but it comes at a cost to the fishery.

Special Regs are the wave of the future. In Washington state, tributaries of the Columbia River are stocked with hatchery rainbow trout (steelhead). These steelies have the adipose fin clipped off before stocking; anglers may take these fish. But native rainbows, with the adipose fin intact, must be released in order to perserve the indigenous race.

Such considerations cover more than concern for the gene pool. Size is also a criteria. Ontario allows only one northern pike larger than 34 inches to be taken per angler per day. Wisconsin recently proposed drawing up special regs for all 10,000 miles of its trout habitat aiming to differentiate those waters where trout are meant for the pan and those meant for picture taking and prompt release. In a few years say some, Minnesota may have 5% of its fishing lakes (200) under catch restrictions.

In addition to size limits on bass for 11 lakes, and on northerns and walleyes for 17 more, Stieger Lake (Carver Co.) is catch-n-release only for all game species. Muskellunge are protected from spearing on 15 designated lakes while a spearing ban on Lake Minnetonka went into effect last year.

A voluntary muskie catch-n-release program called CORE gives muskie fishermen on Leech Lake sew-on patches to honor their non-lethal tactics. A reduction of bag limits for lake trout on soft water lakes is likely because of the relative infertility of these environments and because of the slow growth rates of lakers.

Walleyes are a special category owing to the immense effect - $500 million annualy - this fish has on the state's economy. No detailed agenda is yet available from the DNR's Long Range Planning unit begun in 1987, but there is little doubt special regs will be aimed primarily at the 11 state lakes of 1,000 to 15,000 acres. On these waters, the overall catch rate was 1 walleye per 8.5 hours of fishing as against 1 walleye per every 4.5 hours fishing on the state's 10 lakes larger than 15,000 acres.

Special regulation has long been the byword on trout streams where that fishes' vulnerability has led to rules of etiquette foreign to the lake angler's concept of "total war." But increasingly we as a species are becoming aware of the notion of limits. We may not like it but the days of find'm, fish'm, fillet'm and forget'm are going fast. Perhaps it's time to focus our attention on the poetry of the experience: the play of light on water, the sweet scent of a living world, the serenity and awe of wilderness. We'll still enjoy the sight of a fish, we just won't salivate so much.

Flyer Fever
Raises Midwest's Temperature

Dr. Bob Johnson, a St. Paul, Minnesota, family practitioner, boat collector and host to the annual Weird Boat Rendezvous, wears a t-shirt with the provocative motto: "*Falls Flyers* are like potato chips, you can't stop with just one!"

When ice crystals no longer congregate in automotive fuel lines and the jet stream ceases to divert tundra-fed gales across the state, Minnesotans are likely to witness a phenomenon so intense and widespread that the good doctor's paraphrasing will seem not only prophetic but downright understated. At a point sometime in spring when meltwater and blood are running at approximately the same speed, a small army of collectors, speculators, fad-freaks and just plain folk will fan out over the farms, fields and garage sales of the state in quest of a unique and valuable shard of boating history known as a *Falls Flyer*.

For the *Falls Flyer* Johnson advertises is a special craft, one molded not in the image of Neptune, nor any other denizen of the aqueous depths, but rather after the spirit of *St.Louis!* This sleek, smart-looking speedboat is a tribute to a giant of the air - Charles Lindbergh - one of America's few authentic heroes.

Lindbergh, every Minnesota schoolchild recalls, piloted a single-engine plane across the Atlantic - alone - in 1927, establishing in a single brilliant stroke the future of aviation.

Dr. Johnson's backyard gathering celebrates the rediscovery of this marvelous artifact from the era of American innocence.

In the quixotic history of the speedy *Falls Flyer*, a handmade wooden runabout created to immortalize the grand feat of 'Lucky Lindy', a generation of boomers have found the perfect foil, a means to conjoin their current status with something solid and venerable from their past. Product of genius, victim of war, altered by fire and nearly lost to neglect, the *Flyer* is a phoenix, renewed after decades of indifference, the perfect symbol for a cohort of mid-lifers who have quietly raised families and now seek a new commitment.

That *Falls Flyer* "fever" should strike the Midwest only makes sense, for this nautical antique was born right here on the Mississippi River in the town of Little Falls, some 50-odd years ago. The *Falls Flyer* name in fact is an amalgam of geography - Little Falls - and the state's sole internationally famous son. (The memory of Lindbergh dominates the community even local athletic teams are known as Falls Flyers.)

The story of the *Falls Flyer* begins with Lindbergh's remarkable transit of the open ocean. One of the admiring millions looking on May 21, the date of the historic landing at Le Bourget Air Field, Paris, was Paul Larson, a Lindbergh neighbor in this small central Minnesota town.

Though nine years older, Larson attended the same school and was deeply impressed by his classmate's spectacular achievement.

The Larson who set out to praise the famous aviator in a new line of boats - to be called "Flyer" after Lindbergh and "Falls" for the hometown they shared - was no ordinary tradesman seeking to link his product to a widely advertised name. After all, prior to the moment Lindbergh touched down after his 33 hour, 3,600 mile flight, Larson was the more famous of the two.

And herein lies the tale of a boat too beautiful, too memorable to disappear beneath the waves. Larson's genius figures even larger than the Lindbergh legend in explaining why a boat which once sold for $100 - with motor - can today command a price of $25,000.

Born in Chicago in 1894, Paul Larson ventured with his family to the Land of 10,000 Lakes at the turn of the century when logging in the vast pineries of northern Minnesota reached its zenith. Work in the sawmills adjacent the big log booms of the Mississippi provided for a farm south of Little Falls and it was here that Paul built his first boat, a fishing scow, when just 11 years old. With lumber and nails scavenged from a neighboring farmhouse which burned, he fashioned the craft using a hand-saw, wooden plane and hatchet.

The scow saw action mainly in ditches but Larson persevered. An avid hunter as well as fisherman, he soon designed and built a 14-foot double-ended duck hunting boat that could accommodate two hunters and weighed just 80 pounds. All who saw the boat liked it and orders began to trickle in.

He built the boats in his spare time, steam-bending white oak for ribbing, or smoothing bottom planks by hand, after his shift at the mill. Too poor to buy a boat, and unable to find one to his liking, Larson had become a craftsman and budding entrepreneur while still in his teens.

His big break came when the family moved to land fronting Highway 371, the fabled vacation route between the Twin Cities and Brainerd, water-rich hub of central Minnesota's aquatic playground. Paul made the most of the change in venue, propping up one of his boats outside his shop and reaping a whirlwind of free publicity.

With money from his trap lines invested in power tools, Paul began building 14- and 16-foot boats full-time. By 1922,

The simple Jenny trained Lindbergh and inspired Larson.

83

Larson was the first Johnson outboard motor dealer in the state, packaging his handmade wooden runabouts with Sea Horse motors for a combined price of $100.

Within months of Larson's debut as a Johnson dealer, a young pilot named Charles Lindbergh purchased a celebrated Curtiss biplane, model JN4 - the "Jenny" which trained squads of WWI pilots. Lindbergh barnstormed across the country for the next few years, carrying mail and preparing for the moment that would catapult him into history.

While Lindbergh made his famous crossing in the customized Spirit of St. Louis, well-researched rumor has it that Larson built his *Falls Flyer* line around Lindbergh's aerial prowess in the Jenny.

When production began in 1937, the design of the boat was that of a rounded hull vessel with a double cockpit, built of canvas on wood — the same features as Lindbergh's Jenny, only constructed for performance in a different element.

The identification of the two does not end there, however. Lest anyone overlook Lindbergh's contributions to transportation, Larson built further recognition into the *Flyer*: the original seven inboard prototypes merged port and starboard cutwaters at the bow in the form of a metal Eagle (later changed to a duck, swan or loon) - an unmistakable homage to the 'Lone Eagle.'

The *Flyer* Meant to Conquer Fluid Drag

Larson's other obsession was speed - he was a champion racer in the aerodynamic "Comet", a nearly weightless boat so light he could carry it. What he learned darting along inches above the water translated into the low-slung tapered shape of the *Flyer*.

Larson, in fact, constructed the boat so differently from other boats of the era that in 1940 he took out a patent (his only one in nearly 50 years of boatbuilding) for "a new, original, and ornamental Design for Boats" on the *Flyer*.

"Larson," says Todd Warner, broker of antique (pre-WWII) and classic (post-WWII) boats and cars, "took a helluva risk in designing and building this boat." Warner says that the established wooden pleasure craft of the time - the Hacker-Craft, Gar Woods and Chris Craft - had gone from a round

84

bottom to a V-bottom in the late 1920's with a sharply defined chine or ridge between the sides and bottom spine of the boat. Yet here comes a Flatlander with the daring to "combine round bottom and chine" in a radical new design.

The results were mixed, suggests Warner, who grew up amid *Flyers* on 14,000 acre Lake Minnetonka, a dozen miles west of the Twin Cities. "My 19-foot inboard could go 37 mph, but it would torpedo (sink) if it hit a large wave." Warner sold the boat in 1981 for $7,500 - a fraction of its current value he claims.

Larson apparently appreciated the complexity of the task he had set himself because it seems as if virtually every one of the 25 inboards built varies to some degree. Not only do the lengths differ - 14, 18, 19, 20 and 21-feet - but so do interior color schemes, and size and position of the engine.

Chuck Steele of Madison, Wisconsin, for instance, has a single cockpit *Flyer* with the engine forward; whereas Paul Mikkelson, Hopkins, Minnesota, has just restored a 21-footer with a double cockpit forward; yet Dr. Johnson has an even more unusual placement: cockpits fore and aft with the engine in the middle. Engines vary from a 90 hp. Gray Marine to 140 hp. Gray Fireball.

With half of the inboard type accounted for according to Ross Pfund, *Flyer* chronicler and owner of five *Flyers*, Steele's and Johnson's boats appear to be one-of-a-kinders. Warner notes that subtle hull design differences may mark each boat and have a bearing on their value.

Tom Juul, a much sought-after boat restorer with Alexandria Classic Boats in Alexandria, Minnesota, reiterates the uniqueness of early wooden *Flyers*. "It's totally different from a Chris Craft. The *Flyer* has cedar strip planking and steam bent oak framing, while the Chris Craft has mahogany planking and sawn frames."

Strength-wise, the *Flyer* method has the edge, relates Juul. But the *Flyer* process takes longer and is more difficult, marking it as handmade, while the sawn frames are typical of mass assembly. Cedar stripping makes the boat extremely light, Juul adds, allowing him to pick up and move the stern of an 18-foot inboard by himself.

Juul admits the *Flyer* is partially responsible for a mini-boom in restoration work even if he didn't initially care for the boat Warner describes as a "floating tennis shoe": "I never liked the things until my wife saw a couple at Bob Speltz's annual Albert Lea Boat Show.

"She liked it right away and I figured if she liked it, I should buy one because then she'd let me work on it." Juul, a hobbyist five years ago with only two boats to his commission, is so busy restoring other people's *Flyers* - "we're swamped, I'm booked up three years in advance" - he barely has time to look after his own four *Flyers.*

Juul's been riding a wave of renewed interest in wooden boat construction. "Wooden boats - all wooden boats - are very popular now. People are demanding higher quality restorations; I'm seeing boats that have already undergone two or three restorations and are coming back to have the job completed," he noted.

Credit for the interest in wooden boats among Minnesotans should be divided among several including Warner, who founded the local Land-O-Lakes chapter of the Antique and Classic Boat Society (ACBS) 15 years ago with his Rendezvous Boat Show on Lake Minnetonka, and Speltz of Albert Lea, author of 'the bible' of American powerboating, a six-volume history, *The Real Runabouts.* Until ill-health forced him to abandon his role as long-time ACBS host and *Flyer* aficionado, Speltz helped keep the *Flyer* flame alive. Not to be forgotten of course, is Larson himself.

The radical nature of the *Flyer* flowed from Larson's incessant tinkering as he sought a slender hydrodynamic design with which to pair ever-larger power units. But the problem with a narrow shape was that it tended to spin while cornering.

This difficulty persisted on the inboard models owing to their patented bullet shape and Larson's decision to abbreviate the standard square transom in favor of a revolutionary rounded transom with a contoured rear deck which sloped right to the waterline.

Yet these experimentations were producing phenomenal results on the outboard *Flyers.* Here, the sloping rear deck and rounded transoms were coupled with an extension of the bottom planking several inches beyond the transom. These "stern supports" as Larson called them, pulled the bow up and onto plane in a splash.

In addition to increased balance and stability while cornering, the extra surface area of the stern supports allowed for more weight and bigger motors. Larson's 14-foot Flyers literally flew out of the water to achieve speeds nearly equal to the horsepower of the 35-40 hp. motors propelling them.

Today, of course, rounded transoms, odd-shaped hulls, inclined decks and extended bottoms are virtual standards as the pleasure boat industry follows Larson in the pursuit of acceleration and stability.

Unique too, was the distinctive tri-color paint job of the *Flyers*: after waterproofing the canvas decks with several coats of 'Aeroplane Wing dope', Larson eschewed the traditional varnish finale. Instead, he painted the bottom up to the splash guards in bright red marine enamel, the bow and part of the deck in black with the balance of the boat ivory. All hues blended into delicate ellipses at the bow, suggesting the beak of a bird - perhaps an eagle?

The "aeroplane type cockpits" were upholstered in dark red leatherette; stern, cockpit panel, deck beams and coamings were made of Philipine mahogany. "The *Flyer* was an expensive boat for its time," says historian Pfund.

Riding the crest of post-war recreation, Larson Boats was turning out 2,500 boats, wood and aluminum (under the Crestliner name) each year. But on the morning of December 13, 1949, factory turned inferno as fire swallowed everything: patterns, boat molds, financial records and even Paul's powerboat racing trophies.

Yet Larson managed to transform disaster into triumph. He quickly embraced the new fiberglass technology which promised to make boats smoother riding, stronger, and almost maintainance free. (Aluminum, while longer-lasting than wood, is less flexible and can't be bent to fit forms whereas fiberglass can be shot out of a gun to fit virtually any shape).

Wooden *Flyer* models immediately sprouted "armorglass", a fiberglass coating, and Larson's first molded fiberglass *Flyer* (with a wood-reinforced hull) appeared in 1954.

Though built for three years only - 1955-56-57 - the original design fiberglass *Flyers* ("classical glass" in the Warner parlance) are exceptional. Naturally, Larson didn't take the expedient route of forcing new technology onto old patterns. Instead, he re-sculpted the internal structure of the boat to be much lighter than the competition. Larson thought existing fiberglass boats "felt nailed to the ground."

By 1958 however, Larson had introduced still another novelty: fins. Like the cars of the era, Larson's fiberglass *Flyers* from '58 to '60 - the last year of production - suddenly sprouted dorsal wings on either side of the motor transom diversifying the *Flyer* line with still another collectible quirk.

The hallmark of the *Flyers* in fact, appears to be the rapidity with which Larson felt free to alter the die. It seems almost as if every *Flyer* is unique, a foray into speed and technical mastery as well as a probe into consumer tastes. Restorers report that design continuity does not seem to have been a priority. When a particular vinyl fabric or color ran out, the pattern was simply changed.

In addition to being handmade and eternally experimental, the *Flyer* was subject to a catalog of various factory options as well, one of them being the bizarre egg-shaped motor hood. Offered between 1951 and 1956, the bulky hoods were intended to streamline boat and motor and provide "the appearance of an inboard" according to a Larson brochure. However, the hood did not fit over all motors and required time-consuming exertions to access the starter. As a result, most of the giant egg hoods were discarded with only three originals still surviving according to estimates.

To some degree, Larson's double cockpit idea was inventiveness gone overboard, as the arrangement on the early outboards at least, created two problems: with the steering wheel in the stern compartment, as necessitated by the manual attention required to start pre-war outboard engines, it meant the pilot's straight-ahead vision was blocked if he was so foolish as to bring along passengers in the forward cockpit. Yet without a passenger forward, the *Flyer* lacked good weight distribution and the stern, with motor and pilot, dragged in the water.

Later, as engines came equipped with electrical starting, the steering wheel moved forward. Of course, a single, open cockpit would have eliminated the problem and Larson did build one - only one it seems - perhaps out of loyalty to the double cockpit Jenny.

The "Fever" Breaks

While the U.S. abounds in custom-built boats with unusual features, the *Flyer* was meant to be a stock boat suitable for mass production so far as it went at the time. Alterations of such frequency would normally be avoided in a stock boat but discerning collectors are less exasperated than gleeful at Larson's puttering.

As individuals, *Flyer* owners have long nurtured a secret conviction of the boat's special place in outboard history. They have only recently come out of the boathouse, so to speak, and made their obsession public thanks in part to a chance meeting between Juul of Alexandria and Ross Pfund of Ada, Minnesota.

Pfund had been referred to Juul on another matter when the topic turned to the *Flyer*. The conversation dislodged a flood of childhood memories for Pfund: summertime at his grandparents' lake cabin, playing in the sand along the beach and, of course, the fateful impression made on a youthful mind by the "striking colors" and bullet shape of his first *Flyer* sighting. Pfund, fourth generation editor and publisher of the *Norman County Index*, knew he had a story.

The *Flyer's* wake led to Dr. Johnson, who had kept an informal list of *Flyer* owners obtained through Speltz and his own tenure in the ACBS. By the time Johnson was set to host the first annual *Falls Flyer* Invitational in October, 1989, Pfund launched his own considerable effort on the *Flyer's* behalf.

Titled *Flyer Fever*, Pfund produced a professional-looking, photo-laden newsletter dedicated to gathering the 65-odd members of the *Flyer*-owning clan. With help from a box full of old photos from Lem Larson (Paul's brother and a mechanic for Larson Boats), several first person accounts of *Flyers* discovered and restored, and research into Larson sales brochures, *Flyer Fever* became a 20-plus page quarterly mailed to several hundred people. Most recipients, like the Minnesota Historical Society Library, are non-owner "affiliates."

A year into publication, *Flyer Fever* has spawned a virtual cottage industry in *Flyer* memorabilia, including t-shirts, caps and replica decals. Pfund himself has not only acquired five *Flyers*, but has publicized a vision that encompasses a Vintage Boat museum and an annual *Flyer* Reunion in Little Falls.

One of Pfund's principal functions however, is that of resource center and data gatherer, compiling and analyzing the various pieces of a puzzle dispersed by conflagration and the modern 4-wheel drive. No complete list of owners exists and all early point-of-sale records and serial numbers disappeared in the fire of 1949. Pfund has painstakingly constructed this picture to date:

Some 99 *Flyers* - of all models - still exist with most boats living along an axis from Alexandria, 50 miles west of Little Falls, through Brainerd and thence eastward to the boat country of western Wisconsin. *Flyer* ownership is not confined solely to the Midwest however, with *Flyers* located in Oregon, Ohio, Kansas, Georgia and Pennsylvania.

The wooden inboards, not surprisingly, are the rarest of the species with 12 accounted for out of a possible 25 built.

An equal number of the finned boats - 1958-59-60 - are known to have survived, but Pfund is convinced many more are "out there." Detective work on this one should be simpler owing to Larson's "bold" color schemes: the '58 model made its maiden voyage in basic black. Other choices included red, yellow or white trim and for two years until 1960, the finned *Flyer* came with a peculiar diagonally-striped black-on-yellow bottom.

Some 19 wooden outboards, with and without planing boards ("old" vs. "new style"), are still in existence, displaying all the variety one expects from the fertile Larson imagination.

An inboard, a "finned" model, a hooded engine and the famous fiberglas outboard gather at a '91 reunion.

90

The bulk of extant *Flyers* - some 55 boats as of November 1990 - are fiberglass outboards as befits this nearly indestructible material.

In The Eye of the Beholder

Warner, whose Bristol Classics also acts as general contractor on wooden boat restorations, says the *Flyer* saga demonstrates one of the vagaries of the market where rarity, size and geography all have a part in determining a boat's value. Relative to other boats and other markets, Minnesota's *Flyer* is a "somewhat localized" phenomenon. "The wealthy rare boat collector is generally looking for a wooden boat in the 22-33-foot category and is willing to spend more money than typical for Minnesota," says Warner.

The hottest spot for restoration, explains Warner, is Lake Tahoe where the big 30-foot triple cockpit types have appreciated some 350% in the past 10 years. These "project boats" as Warner calls them, may cost $15,000 and require $25,000 for a complete restoration. Even at that, the value of the boat is probably little more than the cost of restoration - "unless it's very rare." This latter category opines Warner, "will soon see a million-dollar boat."

The restoration itself can be tricky. There is considerable debate over what constitutes "restoration" and when, in fact, "project boats" become "reproductions" which may look like the original but can never sustain the appreciation - financial and otherwise - that comes with the real thing.

Another wooden boat restorer, John Monahan, son of Harold "Bud" Monahan, master mechanic for Larson Boats when Paul was at the helm, is currently restoring seven *Flyers*. He says lengthy research and nationwide contacts are keys to original restoration.

According to Juul, a true restoration should have half of the original wood — a sometimes difficult proposition in light of the fact that most wooden *Flyers* are of an age where the bottoms need to be replaced. Juul says replica hardware is available though the original fixtures are preferable.

Both Juul and Monahan have seen *Flyer* owners show up with unrestorable "junk." And the cost of that junk has gone up like a bad bow rise in recent years: "A few years ago you could pick up a *Flyer* which was pretty much junk for $25-100; you can still find them in deteriorated condition but you'll have to pay $1,200 for it - then put $3,000-4,000 into it (a single 3-foot piece of original cutwater can cost $75)," insists Monahan.

Monahan has personal experience with the speculative fever surrounding the *Flyer*. The 1953 cedar strip outboard his father brought home new for $400 later was sold to a fellow down the street. When Monahan approached the man recently the price had escalated to $8,000.

Monahan believes it's all related to demographics. The baby boomers are coming of age and they want to reclaim a slice of their past: "If it were cars, we would want a '57 Chevy or a '58 Corvette; my dad wanted a Model A."

If there is anyone who epitomizes the myriad concerns - nostalgia, preservation, speculation - that enshrine the *Flyer*, it's Paul Mikkelson, the quintessential victim of "Flyer Fever" with seven of the unusual speedboats. Mikkelson specializes in *Flyers*. He fell in love with the *Flyer* "instantly" he says back in 1956 when his father brought home a new fiberglass double cockpit model.

"The *Flyer* felt good at any speed," he recalls. With a Johnson 30 hp. Javelin on it, the *Flyer* "was great for running through the waves. For the time, the *Flyer* was a fast boat and we did a lot of water skiing with it. I even dated my wife in that *Flyer*."

When his father decided to trade the *Flyer* for a newer boat, Paul bought it from him for $400 and moved it from the family lake cottage to a berth underneath his deck where it remained for the next decade and a half. Just two years ago, Paul decided to restore the boat completely.

"It had picked up some dock scratches through the years and the boat cushions had shrunk from 3 inches to 3/4 inches. I wanted it absolutely new - the way it was when I was a kid." Mikkelson got his wish, a *Flyer* entirely restored to its native splendor, with the exception of a new windshield.

But it did not come cheap. The whole body had to be sanded and some wood replaced; the cutwaters were rechromed; a time-consuming search tracked down the original upholstery on the east coast and he paid a "tremendous premium" to get stainless steel nails that wouldn't rust. Mikkelson says some luck was involved: "I had all the original pieces to start with because no one had ever touched it." And he was fortunate to have the restoration done by John Monahan.

While the restoration cost him nearly 10 times what he paid for the boat, Mikkelson has no second thoughts. "A restoration is always a question of what you're starting with and where you want to go. Sure, you could skip over some details but I'm fussy. The '56 *Flyer* is part of the family, it's for parades and strutting around the lake on Sunday mornings."

Of his other *Flyers* due for restoration, Mikkelson says five will be "pristine" with the other two more accurately described as "partial" restorations. Despite price inflation, Mikkelson has picked up nearly one *Flyer* a month since spring, 1990. He plans on selling several of his current stock, perhaps keeping the rarest, like his 21-foot inboard with its 140 hp. 6-cyl. Gray Marine engine.

Mostly it's a matter of his having formed a deep attachment to the uniqueness and historical claims of the *Flyer*. "My first objective is to keep them from dying. If it was a matter of practicality, you'd go with a modern boat. But if I can keep one alive, even if it doesn't stay with me, then I'll have done something."

Our Dr. Johnson says he too, always liked old boats, enough so to become a member of the ACBS years ago. It was after a meeting of the Society that he bought his first *Flyer*, a rare, 18-foot inboard offered for sale - with motor and trailer - for $600 (before the meet, the ask was $200). When the Juul-restored boat premiered at Lake Tahoe's prestigious Con Cours d'Elegance Boat Show in August, 1991, it was part of a select, invited group of the nation's 100 most expensive and unusual boats. It was also the first time, Johnson laughs, that he had ever ridden in one of his five *Flyers*.

Chapter 4

North Shore

Shore Casting for Salmon

The revival of Lake Superior should be retitled "The Greatest (Fish) Story Ever Told" and pedaled to Hollywood. The scene of course, is unparalleled in terms of raw grandeur and power. The characters (in keeping with La-La Land tradition) are simply drawn: the protagonists are strong, sleek and cold-blooded; the antagonists come from an alien world, are dressed in plastic or rubber and act perpetually hungry.

The action is intermittent yet heart-stopping; and the cast, well the cast is easy once you get into the swing of things. Among the credits for this amazing screenplay are the local and federal managers, scientists and hatchery personnel who contributed their talents.

Once derisively known as the 'Dead Sea' during the 1960's and 70's, Lake Superior has been reborn as the state's most exciting, varied fishery. State and federal fisheries authorities not only conquered the dreaded sea lamprey - a parasitic fish which decimated native lake trout - they repopulated the lake with exotic species within the reach of the average angler.

With the demise of the laker, various niches in the food chain were opened up to other species. The state DNR and the federal Fish and Wildlife Service embarked on a series of experiments designed to provide a fishing stock while the lake trout recovered.

The problem was by no means simple. Lake Superior - especially along the Minnesota coast - is a harsh environment. Superior, the largest freshwater lake in the world, is cold (38 degrees) and deep (to 1,000') with very limited littoral, or shelf, area. It is an oligotrophic (little life lake) without the richness of life spawned by warm shallow waters.

Also, Minnesota North Shore streams are dependent on runoff of rain and snow. They are "flashy," i.e., flowing bank-to-bank on Tuesday, and reduced to a trickle by Friday. Loose gravel at the river mouths is often pushed onshore by storms blocking the rivers when spawners from the big lake are gathering to go upstream. Eggs and fry which manage to make it into the rivers risk being swept downstream during snowmelt and thunderstorms, or killed by drought.

The optimum scenario from a fisheries standpoint, would be a fast-growing anadromous species (running up rivers from the lake to spawn) which took artificial bait readily, fought well when hooked, and possessed a certain marquee charm that fishing audiences would take to. Tryouts were announced and several actors were evaluated.

Steelhead (lake-run rainbow trout) were a popular choice because of their fight and longevity, and because they appear on stage in April, May and June when winter spectators are most in need of entertainment. But steelhead reproduction has been spotty and some years few heed their cue at all. They also are an extremely wary fish and rarely take bait once in the streams.

Other salmonoids (the fish family including salmon, trout and whitefish) auditioned included the Donaldson's, Madison and Kamloops strain of rainbow trout. The Kamloops ('loops in North Shore parlance) was selected because it grew quickly, showed up in time for winter ice action, and demonstrated an indulgence towards anglers stumbling to their seats. Kamloops have also proved to have the highest percentage (5-10%) of return (to stream) of any species stocked in the big lake.

Then there's the gate-crashing pink salmon, or 'humpy', which made its appearance after: a) escaping from a Michigan hatchery; or b) parachuting out of plane bound for a Canadian processing factory. The pink doesn't get very big (3 lbs.) or live much longer than the latest stamp hike, but it fights like Boris Yeltsin and has four-star flavor, the best of all the exotics on the Shore.

Death, of course, is a natural event in the life of Superior and its anadromous fishes. For the muscular chinook, or Pacific king salmon — so strong they can literally swim up rock — doom attends after a brief four years. With stomach atrophied out of existence upon their return to spawning streams, death is certain. This has led to pressure to allow snagging in areas where chinook are so abundant that their mass extinction seems absurd.

Snagging is not a pretty sight: 20# line, 9' spar and, for tackle, a device consisting of a four-pronged treble hook and 6 ounces of lead called an "M-16." With grunts and double-handed swipes, snaggers flog small pools below barriers to upstream migration. Joined should-to-shoulder, a snagger's most frequent contact is another snagger.

When a fish is snagged — it doesn't matter where — it is dragged ashore and gutted in a makeshift abattoir where the waters foam with blood and the banks are stained red. Minnesota officials are determined that so far as possible it does not happen here.

But there is no overlooking this fishes' popularity — not only does the 'ch'nook' make up 90% of the excitement allowed by the AMA, it also provides a source of meat in a community which has seen its share of economic hardship. If the Superior ecosystem is going to be exploited, why shouldn't it benefit those who have invested their equity year around?

To diffuse some of the adulation - and potential controversy - surrounding the chinook, the coho, or silver salmon, was added to the script. The coho is even more short-lived than the chinook (3 yrs) but hits artificials with greater alacrity and has "naturalized" itself, in the words of Don Shriner, Lake Superior Fisheries Manager.

Using the broad, deep rivers of Canada and Wisconsin, the coho has established a breeding population and are the second most abundant fish in the lake, says Shriner, after the resurgent lake trout. The coho are so successful, the Minnesota DNR no longer stocks them. Coho come onshore in November and December, after the September arrival of the chinook, and just in time to give the more hearty angler an excuse to visit 'the Lake.'

Another contender to the lead role is the Atlantic salmon, a sleek silvery torpedo of a fish inducted into Lake Superior in 1980. The Atlantic live 10-15 yrs. in their native ocean environment (possibly less in Superior) making several spawning runs. The fact that an angler may decide to release an Atlantic knowing it may still grow, reduces pressure for a put-n-take fishery.

While chinook now returning to the North Shore average 12 lbs. (8-10 for the Atlantic vs. 3 for coho) some 15 lb. Atlantic have been picked up and their potential is thought to be 20 lbs. More importantly, Atlantic salmon are spectacular aerial fighters and, when stocked in inland lakes, feed near the surface during summer months while other inland trout - lakers or brookies - remain deep and inaccessible.

The long-range status of the Atlantic however, remains in doubt. While a gifted performer, the Atlantic has a somewhat tarnished reputation as a temperamental talent. Because of its inbred inability to tolerate overcrowding - it's more territorial and won't stack up like other salmon species according to Lee Peterson, supervisor of Atlantic brood stock - the Atlantic needs more space and a more specific diet. Both demands add up to an expensive actor.

The Atlantic was intended to be a "trophy" fish in Shriner's words, fun for the angler but not a reliable "everyman" for the locker. Even so, returns have been disappointingly slim - less than .1% - of fish released.

Shriner says the role of the Atlantic has to be looked at critically in light of its record of no-shows. He admits that while not all reviews are in, the Atlantic, and declining Chinook numbers, might well be victims of the successful reappearance of the lake trout.

Laker numbers, he notes, are at an all-time high. "You can't expect salmonoids to compete evenly with lake trout - they weren't made for this aquatic system, so it's not surprising they would be the first losers in this group of fishes."

It's true, lakers do have the advantage. The native Isle Royale strain - historically fewer in numbers than the Sisikit strain from Lake Michigan - are believed to have withstood the lamprey scourge rather well. Within casting distance from shore during July and August, lakers spawn on distant offshore reefs beyond the reach of most fishermen.

Their return, says Shriner, though it may mean fewer salmonoids, is, after all, a triumph of conservation - saving the native species - "and that's what fish management is all about."

Enter the Antagonist

Every play needs a villain and, if our finny friends are the 'heroes' of the Superior saga, we - those who would catch and cook them - must fill that role. But, as they say in playwriting circles, 'the villain always has more fun.'

It's true. For real fun - no more fishing off the dock for sunnies or despairing of ever catching a walleye with as much fight as an Iraqi conscript - fish Superior. And if you think an 18' deep-V package is necessary, read the script again. The whole point of clogging the lake with salmon was to bring fish within reach of those on shore — the "groundlings", or common people of Shakespeare's day.

That's right, it's the shore fisherman who fills out the cast and has all the fun.

River fishing when the "run" is on, say on the Lester in Duluth, or the Baptism further up the shore, resembles a scene from "Boyz 'N the Hood." Annoying too, is stream etiquette requiring one to strong-arm a strike to the surface in order to determine whether it is fair or foul hooked (elsewhere than the mouth).

Stream fishing can be a crowded affair during the "run."

And suppose you're just a tad too old to plod miles along the muddy banks of a strange river only to have someone jump in beside you after finally finding the 'perfect' spot.

Well, the answer is shore casting, a piece of theater tailor-made to combine action, adventure and beauty — as well as some pretty hefty fillets.

Shore casting is an active part, no staring at bobbers or reclining while 95 horses do the work; a firm drag and knowing one's lines are essential.

Shore casting differs from stream fishing in several respects: Stream fishing for chinook demands stout rods and heavy line to stem the surges of the big exotics before they turn downstream and are lost among snags, deadfalls and the legs of other anglers. In such an event, drama becomes tragedy or slapstick as the unfortunate angler either gives up his fish or plunges after it in a clownish display.

Shore casting goes lighter, from 6# line and a 9' graphite fly rod, down to 4# or even 2# test and a shock absorbing 11' "noodle" rod. The longer rods give more casting distance while sacrificing brute strength which is less important in the Lake, an expansive environment where 250 yards of line can be yielded (and probably will) by the fisherman with no loss in advantage.

Stream fishing is an "iffy" venture: today the stream gives a lackluster performance, it is low, warm and empty; tomorrow, due to an inland rain, it is high, fast and filled with salmon, lakers and 'humpies', but you don't have a ticket and the crowd is SRO.

Meanwhile, shore casters have been applauding one encore after another as stream migrators school offshore, waiting for conditions to favor their upstream advance. In fact, shore casters can pretty much expect some hungry species will be patrolling within reach for the eight months of open water.

During "the run", a stream may become choked with salmon but those anglers who land fish may discover to their dismay, that the star is "spawned out", i.e.,black skinned, not silver, with soft, yellow flesh not suitable for the table. Casters on the other hand, have miles of stable, dry footing at their disposal and each hooked fish is still full of fight and savor.

Hooking a salmon is a difficult affair for the stream fisherman as well. The small yarn flies used must drift along the bottom the same speed as the current. Often the delicate pick-up of the fish goes undetected except by the patient, skilled and lucky angler. Unfortunately, many times the hook will have found the wrong part of the fish; the salmon must be released if the hook is embedded anywhere except the mouth, that's the law.

Shore casters are not hassled with these details. Snags are a rarity (the inexperienced will lose tackle to the rocky bottom until they get the exact count) since the cast is made over water 10-20' deep.

The shore caster does not have to be on the bottom because Lake Superior predators attack their prey from below. (Many shore casters replace factory trebles with a single #1 siwash hook which is not only easier to disengage from hubcap-sized boulders, but also much stronger).

Shore casters also have it over their streamside counter-parts in their choice of baits and the hours in which fish are accessible. Stream fishermen may use a single salmon egg or sack of eggs called a spawn bag, but generally go with bits of colored yarn (the "hot" color may vary from stream to stream or day to day depending on conditions) cut to resemble an egg because they stay on the hook better.

Few lures are employed streamside on the highly selec-tive spawners as trebles cannot be used on North Shore streams. And the stream angler can begin his campaign no earlier than an hour before sunrise and must furl his standards no later than an hour after sunset — missing what are considered the most productive hours.

Casters into Superior face virtually no limits except possession: 10 chinook (about 200 lbs.) and 3 Atlantic salmon. Fishing the big water is continuous with no season except for lake trout; choice of baits appears to be inexhaustible. However, the experts do advise certain stratagems:

Jack Povaser, famed on the Shore for popularizing night fishing, suggests looking for fins breaking the surface during a light breeze, a strong onshore NE wind however, means "they won't be jumping, they'll go up the river mouths if there's enough water. That's when I'll use spawn anchored just off the bottom with split shot." (Some casters add a pea-sized ball of styrofoam to a spawn bag to keep it off rocks.)

If the river is high and a plume of turbid water forms at the mouth as after a heavy fall rain, Povaser goes to a large floating rebel or rapala highlighted with phosphorescent paint — "The bigger baits catch the bigger fish — especially when fishing at night." He adds this advice, "I don't want it too bright, I like to give it 10-15 minutes of casting before I flash it again with the light."

If stream mouths are low, or blocked, and the Lake is clear, Povaser will go to either a tiny, O-sized copper Mepps spinner or a nightcrawler - all in low-light conditions.

Bob Carlson, a Duluth guide who figures he's caught hundreds of chinook, claims the crucial ingredient for shore casters is a light (5-10 mph) onshore breeze either NE or SE, "if you've got wind, you've got fish. The onshore wind blows warm water (48-50 degrees is perfect) in; the worst condition is a strong NW wind which blows warm water out."

Carlson, pinpointing the best shore casting spots near Duluth, suggests the old Curling Club site (Leif Erickson Park), the pumping station (south of Brighton Beach Rd.), Stony Pt. (adjacent Tom's Lumber Camp) off Scenic Hiway 61, and most any of the river mouths from the Lester to the Cascade.

Bob Crom of Sportsman's Headquarters, 17 West Superior Street in downtown Duluth, advises shore casters to be alert for seagulls feeding on baitfish near the surface and in-coming weather fronts with falling atmospheric pressure as indicators.

Crom recommends acquiring a few props: a mid-size to large spinning reel with a minimum spool capacity of 200 yds of 6-8# quality monofilament. A 5:1 gear ratio is a necessity, says Crom, for a smooth, rapid retrieve preventing the lure from sinking toward Davy Jone's locker. He favors crocodiles, loco spoons, cleos, kastmasters, etc, in 3/8 to 7/8 oz. sizes with blue, silver and pearl prism for clear water conditions and chartreuse, gold and orange for cloudy water.

Casting paraphernalia does not end there however, with waders a prerequisite to gain the additional 20-30' that puts the angler in touch with offshore troughs typical of river mouth topography. Neoprene-insulated waders are best suited for Superior's icy waters (with felt-soled boots about $150), but you can beef up that pair of canvas waders picked up at a garage sale with neoprene booties ($20) and polypropylene long johns to keep moisture away from the skin.

Layers of wool or down are obligatory as is a stocking cap for any extended tour of the salmon's wintry domain.

For those who wish to get even closer to the action, Crom suggests a belly boat or float tube, a one-man raft that can be steered, via fins, out into the lake for even greater coverage ($150).

A few swivels, a couple of baggies to separate spoon sizes and a thermos of hot coffee completes the shore caster's ensemble. Well, almost. There's still the fish: a potpourri of adrenal thrills as one morning a school of 2-3 lb. rainbows strike repeatedly; another day, a large lake trout engages a custom-made Sage graphite rod (Jim's Bait, 319 E. 14th St., Duluth) in a dawn tug-of-war; inevitably, a desperate encounter with the brawny salmon, scaly pit bull of this, the pinnacle of Great Waters.

Shore casters revel in a special relationship with the environment being literally up to their knees in the magic well of Lake Superior. When not tangling with the Lake's mighty predators or rubbing a sore shoulder, the shore caster may find himself upstaged by the infinite repertoire of that marvelously gifted showman, Mother Nature: now a shadowy outline of an ore carrier as it slips through the refrigerated mists bubbling up from the depths of this inland sea; later, glowing pink and yellow auroras pulsate across a black velvet sky.

All the while sapphire and turquoise hues tumble in the melted crystal crest of a wave, and golden eyes or mergansers wing inches above the foam at 50 mph.

Shore casters share the limelight willingly. The $5 admission fee they've paid to enter the Superior theater guarantees them a spotlight when the curtain goes up. Now, how could Hollywood pass up a chance to direct such a major motion picture?

Superfish

Fisheries biologist Eric. R. Anderson is balancing on the deck of a 21-foot powerboat peering into the roiling, chocolate-colored waters of the St. Louis River south of Duluth. Using receiver, headphones and a hefty aluminum antenna, Anderson has spent days cruising whirlpools and eddies for sounds of a dozen lithium batteries attached to a very special fish - the sturgeon.

Today, Anderson and fisheries technician Rory Friermuth have fought the St. Louis for three hours, carefully pushing upriver against the powerful tide below Fond du Lac Dam while listening for a delicate "plip, plip" signal from the tiny batteries. Just now the boat swings in the current opposite Chambers Grove Stockade west of the Hwy. 23 bridge - the exact spot where the fish and the $165 batteries were dropped weeks ago.

After several such trips, Anderson has drawn some conclusions: Four of the fish, he presumes, have drifted downstream into Lake Superior; seven more are spread out in the 20 riverine miles between the big lake and the stockade, and one fish is still missing. Without hesitating, Anderson motions Rory to continue - upstream. It's not the $165 batteries that inspire such diligence, but the fact they are attached to a legend, an amazing form of life not seen in any numbers on this stretch of water for more than 100 years.

Anderson is hoping to get a glimpse of the two-pound, 24-inch juvenile lake sturgeon he raised at a Waterville, Minn., hatchery since the time a score of them fit cozily in a tablespoon.

Sturgeons comb the bottom in search of what Anderson says is the good kind of cholesterol: crayfish, fingernail clams, aquatic worms and insect larvae. But anything on the bottom seems to be fair game, and sturgeon stomachs have contained some pretty strange items, including a bushel of onions, a dead cat, rifle bullets, pocket knives, coins and combat medallions from World War I. One Minnesotan who tried to raise them found adults did very well on a diet of oats and barley. In fact one sturgeon's stomach held 66,000 immature midges. Sturgeons suck in all of this food through toothless mouths.

The results of all this eating are big fish, of whalelike size in some parts of the world. The largest, the beluga sturgeon of the Caspian Sea, can reach 28 feet in length; the white sturgeon, West Coast cousin of Minnesota's lake sturgeon, weighs as much as a draft horse. (One of the rare exceptions to this wealth of growth hormone is the shovelnose, or hackleback sturgeon, a native of Minnesota, which may reach only 15 pounds).

While not quite as majestic as belugas, our own lake sturgeon nevertheless is impressive: The Minnesota angling record (and world record, according to the Fishing Hall of Fame, Hayward, Wis.) for a lake sturgeon, caught in September, 1987, is 92 pounds; a 236-pounder was netted off Long Point, Lake of the Woods, in 1936, and a still larger lake sturgeon, 310 pounds, was netted in Chequamegon Bay, Lake Superior, in 1911.

Stories of 400-pounders told by Great Lakes commercial fishermen of the last century, and an 1854 account written by some Wadsworth fellow who claimed to have witnessed a colossal sturgeon swallow an Indian lad named Hiawatha - and his canoe - have not been confirmed.

The adventure of angling for a hooked sturgeon is second to none. Eric Anderson likens it to "deep-sea action," and long-time sturgeon fisherman Joel Anderson of Mahtomedi says muskies and salmon simply don't compare with the sturgeon for power and endurance. "Most people are not prepared to land a big sturgeon. It's a tackle buster; a sturgeon will wear out a good man."

The holder of the state record, Jim DeOtis of Maple Grove, concurs: "A sturgeon will fly several feet out of the water like a bass, fight more stubbornly than a catfish, cleverly hunt the shallows for something to break the line or roll up and cut it with its scutes" (if it is still young enough to have the sharp scutes on its back).

DeOtis, who uses a small hook baited with worms, has such respect for the sturgeon's reluctance to part with its freedom that he previews a likely pool to remove deadfalls the fish will undoubtedly use to its advantage. He admits his record fish - two hours in the landing on 15-pound test - is not the last word in trophy sturgeon. "There are bigger fish out there, some over 200 pounds. They just don't get landed."

Cooked, sturgeons command equal attention for their firm white meat with texture and taste compared favorably with chicken or veal, depending whether it is smoked, cut into strips and baked, or served the way the Indians did, grilled over alderwood. Sturgeon is an oily meat, so some cooking methods may be inappropriate; from ancient Rome to nouvelle cuisine in Los Angeles, the best houses offer it fresh broiled with herb butter. They may offer another form of sturgeon even more celebrated - caviar.

Arranged in loosely wound coils by the millions, and perhaps amounting to a quarter of the female's weight, sturgeon eggs are a creation for the fantasy as much as the tongue. In order to be processed, the eggs must be gathered a critical few hours before they soften and are released. They are then pressed through a sieve to remove blood, fat and membranes, soaked in brine and introduced to mysterious spices resulting in hors d'oeuvres that are savored, not chewed; experienced, not consumed.

However, the roe of the Minnesota lake sturgeon cannot be sold and can be taken only as a consequence of angling.

Lake sturgeons were once very abundant in virgin Minnesota. Their spawning runs choked rivers, their eggs coated both banks for great distances, even the sounds of their spawning ritual - hurling their huge bulks out of the water, landing with a thunderous crash - could be heard up to a mile away. Their range extended over each of the three great basins that grow from this state: Hudson's Bay, the St. Lawrence River and the Mississippi. Lake of the Woods carried the title "sturgeon pond."

The Ojibways honored the sturgeon, calling it "water buffalo" because its size could sustain the appetites of entire families. But the growing white population of the territory, beginning with the first treaty of 1837, did not share the views of prior management.

The sturgeon was a nuisance, tangling and ripping nets set for whitefish, lake trout and walleyes, more valuable species then. Whenever possible, especially during spring mating runs when they entered water only a few inches deep, sturgeons were set upon, clubbed, speared, hacked and dragged up on shore to be set afire or used for hog chow. Their only use for human consumption was by slaves, Indians and, with their gift for nuance, the French.

The annihilation of the sturgeon, begun in hatred and ignorance, was nearly acccomplished by love and attention. The earlier settlers may have been ignorant of the fish's potential - a traveler to Niagara Falls in 1791 calling it "a bad, useless sort of fish" - but later arrivals from Europe brought a broader perspective.

Since the coming of William the Conqueror, the common people of England were forbidden to fish sturgeons, but in colonial America sturgeons were not only unprotected, they also swam in seemingly inexhaustible numbers. After stocks of the East Coast's Atlantic sturgeon were plundered to near extinction, sturgeon hunger moved into the Great Lakes and waylaid the lake sturgeon.

Beginning with the first sturgeon-processing factory at Sandusky, Ohio (1855), and lasting for about 50 years until the last profitable corpses were hauled out of Lake of the Woods, sturgeon netting on the Great Lakes was the path to riches.

Nor was demand limited to flesh and eggs. Science devised remarkable uses for the sturgeon.

Isinglass, a gelatinlike substance made from the fish's swim bladder, was used as a clarifying agent in beer and wine; it also acted to stiffen jams and jellies. Glue was made from the large, bony head. The fatty carcass was rendered, and the oil put to work in paints. Finally the skin of the sturgeon could be tanned and formed into fashionable leather.

A single 6-foot female fish weighing around a hundred pounds could be worth a month's wages when payment for eggs was computed. Keep in mind, that's a month's wages the hard way--a 60-hour work week was standard in 1890.

In 1880, 5 million pounds of sturgeon were taken out of Lake Erie, 4.3 million out of Lake Michigan. Fish populations fell rapidly under such pressure which rolled like a dangerous wave toward the western shore of Lake Superior and the St. Louis River.

In about 1885, 10,000 pounds of sturgeon were pulled from the rapids upstream of Fond du Lac. Superior, however, differs considerably from the other Great Lakes, being colder, much deeper and more infertile. Only 7 percent of it is shoal area, the 5 to 30 feet depths that sturgeons prefer. They were never plentiful in the big lake, and soon they were gone. Inland, along the Little Fork and Rainy rivers, they still collected by the thousands.

By 1888, Lake of the Woods was already yielding four times as much as the highest poundage recorded from the St. Louis. The harvest grew at an astonishing clip, with the years 1893 to 1896 each producing more than a million pounds of undressed fish.

The importance of the sturgeon to the local economy during these boom years and its effect on the imagination requires description: Along the border of Itasca and St. Louis counties is 2,000-acre Sturgeon Lake; flowing northwest out of the lake, the Sturgeon River slides through Sturgeon River State Forest on its way to Sturgeon Township, then past the village of Sturgeon, where it lies within miles of Sturgeon Portage on Lake Vermillion.

Being a big fish in a small pond, as many have discovered, has its disadvantages, and, by 1909, only 34,000 pounds of a once vast spawning population could be located at the mouth of Rainy River. By 1922 all commercial fishing for sturgeons in Minnesota was banned, but experts believe the ban came too late. It is estimated that today the Minnesota sturgeon fishery is less than 1 percent of its former abundance.

A similar disaster occurred throughout the lake sturgeon's range: extinct in Alabama and Georgia, endangered (close to extinction) in nine other states and threatened (in decline) according to the Department of the Interior, in Minnesota.

This explains Anderson's willingness to push the slender craft upstream into the seasonal rundown from the pool above the Fond du Lac Dam.

That one unaccounted-for sturgeon with a battery in its tummy represents a significant part of the effort to bring sturgeon back to the prominence they enjoyed and the waters they ruled. Anderson and the batteries are trying to fathom some of the mysteries of sturgeon - is the St. Louis suitable habitat, or will sturgeon migrate to Superior?

With its lake sturgeon in trouble, Minnesota was eligible for support from the U.S. Fish and Wildlife Service's Anadromous Fish Conservation Act, and Anderson, who has spent his professional life trying to make big, healthy fish from caviar, was happy to help out.

Other fish may have life expectancies of only a few years and mature rapidly and reproduce frequently so their numbers can grow quickly as long as environmental conditions remain favorable.

But sturgeons are made for the long haul, explains Anderson. "They don't have a life span in the human sense; one sturgeon was known to have lived 156 years." Anderson estimates Jim DeOtis' record fish at "60 to 70 years," so his 5-foot-9 fish was still growing.

In keeping with the deliberate pace of its existence, a female sturgeon - tallied in human terms - would graduate high school, get her driving license, take her first apartment and probably make a career change, all before her first stirring of sexual interest. Nor, it appears, is there much appeal in the male of the species, for females spawn at lengthy intervals, often four to seven years. As one might suspect, the egg is the most trying stage in the life of a sturgeon.

For two years, while he scouted for gravid (pregnant) sturgeons in Minnesota, Anderson obtained eggs from the Wisconsin Department of Natural Resources.

Anderson doesn't believe it's good for Minnesota to depend on importing Wisconsin seed, but he's had little luck within the St. Croix system, and a month on the Loon River revealed spawners, but also disturbing evidence of poaching - piles of .22 caliber shells littering the bank, and post holes visible in the mud where set lines had been placed at night.

Whether poaching for their own lockers or sale outstate, poachers pose a very serious threat to a sturgeon renaissance. "This area is too large to be policed by COs (conservation officers)," says Anderson. "Big sturgeon are easy targets. They are also the only hope we have of establishing a thriving native population."

When females in spawning readiness are found, a crew must be at hand to deliver the eggs caesarean and mix them with milt from the males. At this point in the natural scheme of things, the eggs become extremely adhesive, sinking to the stream bed and attaching to rocks instead of drifting downstream into the mouths of carp and suckers. If not treated with bentonite, a claylike substance used to overcome this adhesiveness, the egg masses bind together, suffocating most.

Then there is the gauntlet of fungal infections, water-temperature calibrations, critical diet changes and puzzling maladies of which Anderson has only too painful acquaintance: The entire '86 crop of 75,000 half-inch fry was lost owing to a bizarre sequence of mechanical mishaps. It was a setback, but the program had two more years to run, and Anderson managed about 5,500 plantings before the accident. Many of these 12-to-14 inch fish are still in the St. Louis, and some are being caught and returned to the water as required by the statewide 45-inch minimum-size limit.

Young sturgeon can be handled easily, almost one might think liking it.

Anderson is confident that the goal of a self-sustaining population of sturgeons for the St. Louis is attainable. Yet, while those 5,000-plus sturgeons have beaten odds of a million to one in the wild just to escape the egg, he is not satisfied.

The Soviet Union has 27 beluga hatcheries, and California has a program releasing 500,000 white sturgeons annually into San Francisco Bay.

There are many initiatives Anderson would like to pursue, from sample nettings in other rivers to wider demand feeding that might accelerate sturgeon maturity by five or six times, as has been proven elsewhere. But developing a conscience in support of the sturgeon is not easy.

Budget, staff and space are limited. Although Anderson presented slide shows to a half-dozen fishermen's groups, he faced the brick-wall realities: "With little angling interest, it's hard to get the government involved in raising sturgeon, but without very many sturgeon out there to catch there can be little angling interest."

Harvestable colonies of lake sturgeons are found elsewhere in the state, most notably in the St. Croix and its tributaries, the Snake and Kettle rivers. A few legal sturgeons (in the 20- to-25-pound class) are picked up each season in Red Lake, Lake of the Woods and both shores of Superior.

So far the St. Louis River is the only beneficiary of Minnesota's modest stocking program for sturgeons. There are good reasons why Anderson has chosen to reward this stream, for like the lake sturgeon itself, the St. Louis was mugged and left for dead at the turn of the century.

It is a familiar story: a wild and beautiful river degraded to a conduit for sewage in the years when "progress" was the only priority.

Accounts from the early 1800s telling of "vast" amounts of walleye, pike and sturgeon, enough so that no one went hungry, could hardly be believed in contrast to the dead trough of filth 35 separate polluters had made of the river. Eventually only bullheads and carp swam in the river while sludge worms crawled over the bottom debris of wood fiber and pulp. Only a few sturgeon sightings were reported in this century.

Priorities changed in the 1960s, and the Clean Water Act of 1965 and subsequent amendments mandated a new regional treatment center for human and industrial wastes. With the giant sanitation facility completed in Duluth by 1979, the St. Louis began to flush itself. First, large numbers of spawning walleyes showed up, then the health notices, foul odors and gas bubbles disappeared. Now maybe it's time for the lake sturgeon's return.

Suddenly Anderson is clutching the headphones. He has picked up No. 12 out there in the churning waters at the periphery of the telemetry signal. He urges Rory forward into the pounding current while he strains to strengthen the echo. They proceed cautiously in the 4-to-5-foot depths, the 75-horsepower engine moaning, bow twisting left and right. Just ahead, around the corner, a flood of rust-colored water stampedes through open sluices. It's dangerous as well as impossible to go any farther, but Anderson has at last locked in the signal.

This two-pound bundle of muscle is swimming upstream and is now nearly below the dam. The headphones come off, and the boat turns and sails downstream. It is a satisfying moment. Really big sturgeons, those of myth and legend, seek out deep holes, often below large dams, safe from human predators. This little fellow has returned to the home of its ancestors. Anderson smiles. "A lot of people are showing an interest in sturgeon now. They're waking up to the fact that it's a pretty neat fish."

Charting Superior

The quick, easy way to tap the growing fishing potential of Minnesota's inland sea, Lake Superior, is by charter. Some 12 different charter boats are available just off Lake Ave. in Duluth's Waterfront Plaza Marina. We chose Capt. Richard Arganbright's 27' Crestliner, the Reel-Fish-In.

Along for the expedition were Jim and Peggy Thompson of Appleton, MN, and their two boys, David and Brent; our photographer was Gerard Strauss of Edina. Capt. Arganbright welcomed us aboard at 3 pm and we were soon underway, sliding past the retired Great Lakes ore carrier, the William A. Irvin (open for tours), under the famous Aerial Lift Bridge and into the Duluth entry channel where hundreds were lined up to watch the passage of mighty ocean-going vessels. With the tea-stained waters of the harbor basin behind us, the Captain revved up the 260 hp MerCrusier engine to 27 mph and handed the

Leaving the Duluth entry canal, the captain opens the throttle.

113

wheel over to First Mate son Dennis. Our destination was the Pumping Station four miles up the North Shore.

While he readied the lines, Capt. Arganbright talked fishing. A licensed charter guide the past two years, he's actually fished Superior for 17, ever since the lamprey scourge was checked in the early 1970s and Minnesota and Wisconsin DNRs began restocking with Lake trout and salmon species.

He'd seen it all: clouds of 'mystery fish' on the sonar that no one could catch (they turned out to be carp); summers so hot and dry the salmon concentrated in dense schools where a boat could pick its limit in a couple of hours; sterile brown trout with strange coloration topping 12 lbs.; spring spawning runs thick enough to bring out 200 boats; and rapid weather changes where turned-on fish suddenly smacked everything in the water. Today, he'd see more oddities served up by the Great Lake.

The plan was to run two lines per person, most of them attached to deep downrigger balls at 105' for Lake trout since most salmon had departed the area after good fishing in May and June and before their return in August for fall spawning. Two lines would be rigged on Dipsy Divers (weighted planers) at 48-50' where the video sonar showed occasional large silhouettes - possibly solitary coho or chinook or even Atlantic salmon resting on the thermocline between warmer surface water and colder bottom layers.

Two lines would be set on planer boards 30' or so to either side of the boat to run within a few feet of the surface in order to entice top-water feeders. This had been a very productive technique according to the captain 'til a few days before when a major insect hatch had died away. In addition, 'sliders' - spoons fastened above deeper lines by means of leaders and rubber bands - would complement existing sets and provide complete coverage of the water column.

The rods were heavy duty Diawa downriggers; the reels Penn and Diawa level-winds with 14# test mono, except for one tortuous device armed with 600' of stainless steel wire and a 1# weight. This rod bounced along the bottom to catch (or render unconscious?) anything that had taken refuge there. The deeper lines were dressed with squid imitations and frozen smelt; mid-level lures were of the Bomber type; surface lures were jointed Rapalas. The table was set, all we had to do was catch 'em.

By the time we had completed our first pass arriving off the Lakeview Castle some nine miles from downtown Duluth, our dreams of early success had evaporated. Temperatures were in the 80's with no wind and the big lake was flat as an ironing board. "They're there, we'll have to work for 'um," is all the Captain would allow. It would be another hour before the first strike.

We'd run out of questions to ask Capt. Arganbright and were no longer planning just how to broil a 23-pounder when the fish hit. "There's one!" Arganbright shouted. We hadn't established any iron-clad pecking order and had, in fact, lost track of which rods should have been bowed with the weight of downriggers and which belonged upright behind the planing boards.

Finally, the Captain, who advertises "you set the hook" pointed out the correct rig and Jim grabbed it and pulled back. But the fish had tasted steel and spit the hook leaving only a mangled smelt. "Gotta be quick," Arganbright said quietly.

I deemed myself next in line and took a ready position near the transom. When Arganbright pointed at one of the dozen rods and said, "There's another," I was prepared. Unfortunately, the fish chose the wire line. It was hooked but the line and the lead weight were so heavy (I might have been squeezing the rod a bit tightly as well) I was hurting as much as my adversary.

Reeling in an 1/8 mile of steel line and sinker - plus fish - from 20 fathoms was more work and less fun than imagined. Forearm burning and fingers numb I'd begun to wish for less of a burden when the fish, whatever it was, obliged dropping off at the precise moment it should have broken the surface and rendered at least a visual reward for all that effort. "Biting light today," the Captain said sympathetically.

Photographer Strauss, who had taken a roll of preliminary shots and now had little to do but aim at stray clouds, got the call on the third take minutes later. But again, by the time he'd reeled in the slack and set the hook, Mr. Laker had administered another lesson in elusive behavior. Our expedition was interrupted at this point by a brief northwest squall.

As other charters headed for shore, Capt. Arganbright got on the marine band for up-to-date radar information. "Sure would like to get you people some fish," he said between calls.

Even though the rough weather - 40 mph gusts - made it difficult to maintain course over a trench a mile from the mainland, Captain persevered once assured the wind and light rain wouldn't last the hour. But by 8:30 as a crimson glow from the setting sun fanned toward us from the west, even Arganbright was willing to call it quits.

As he set about drawing in the lines, he suddenly exclaimed, "Whoa, here's one!" The rod was handed to David who succeeded in boarding a 3 lb. laker. Before reaching the ship canal, First Mate Dennis pointed out dense patterns of fish below the boat prompting another pass. The planer rod bent forward and Brent had a fish, a walleye. "Never caught one of those before," commented the Captain. Moments later another hit and Peg had a second nice walleye.

Arganbright, who had now been on the water for 16 straight hours - long enough to take on a resemblance to Capt. Quint of "Jaws" - shook his head, "The lake's never the same, every day is different." He might have added, 'and you have to set the hook'.

Highway 61 Revisited

North of Grand Marais on Highway 61, beyond the tiny hamlet of Hovland and due west of Double Bay, one is bound to notice a strange notch on the Superior Ridge 500' above the great lake. Sprouting from solid rock like an all-weather mushroom is the unfinished abode of James Michael McCanney.

By all accounts Mr. McCanney is something of an eccentric — westerly winds coming over the ridge reputedly can top 100 mph and the unrailed deck constitutes the first step in an IDS-sized tumble. There is even the vaguest whisper among the cedar and poplar bending to the stiff breezes that wrap the crest of the ridge, that Mr. McCanney has constructed his utopian retreat not only on the edge of space but also on the periphery of legality.

The controversy over the cabin helps explain its vexing state of incompletion. Mr. McCanney did not run out of funds or desire so much as he is suffering a temporary deficit of goodwill — just the sort of mortar which makes up for so much else in this remote community. As events stand now, only the hawks can reach his aerie with ease.

Begun in 1986 on a portion of his 40 acres that rockets off the major tract like a satellite, the wood-frame chalet-style house has not seen a hammer in three years, the approximate span his neighbors have closed the gate on materials. This is not to say McCanney cannot reach the wooden shell that outlines his dreams for those who pass below on the highway.

If he wishes he can ascend a tortuous, foot-wide game path or risk the 45 degree-angle ATV trail up the stone face of

Farquhar Peak (elev. 1250') allowed him by the U.S. Forest Service.

But McCanney, a former computer engineer with NCR Comten in Roseville, does not want to scale the vast height like a mink or embark on a dangerous solo trip via three-wheeler. He wants to haul the windows, paneling and insulation necessary to complete the chalet and invite occasional guests without hiring Sherpa to guide them. It will not be easy for, in building the foundation to his lofty paradise, McCanney fabricated some fairly grandiose problems as well.

The act of creation comes easy for McCanney — so too does nonconformity. In high school, while others smoothed their opening lines or searched for facial hair, McCanney reportedly bent ash boughs into snow-shoes (in July) and built a steel cross-bow. After graduate school at Tulane University, he crafted knotty pine furniture. Teaching mathematics in Puerto Rico he fashioned a wooden sailboat using 100 year-old "purple- hearted" timbers for his keel.

Later, as an instructor at Cornell University in Ithaca, New York, he challenged the mouthings of astronomy bigwig, Carl Sagan, and suddenly found himself back in Minnesota selecting Lake Superior boulders for a fireplace in his first cabin, a two-room affair, below the ridge, made from logs he felled, stacked, split and finished.

Despite his lengthy perambulations, McCanney, who was born in Ely, Minnesota, claims to be a local boy whose long-term ambition was to build an airy perch on the sliver of his property which rose perpendicular to the world so high as to give him a 50 mile vista on Lake Superior — far enough to encompass Isle Royale on a clear day.

In the spirit of live and let live which, he says, used to pervade Hovland, he appropriated an old logging road off Cook County 71 on the north slope of the Superior Ridge for his use in constructing the new cabin. Although he did not ask permission - he says the road wasn't posted then - he did not hide his presence either and expected to negotiate any difficulties with individual landowners as they arose.

The access through Moose Valley served very well for bringing in 2x4s and fiberboard, so well the house was half-finished before Kenneth Torstad, the man who built the road

Unfinished gem or done-for eyesore?

and maintains a "semi-residential" dwelling on the ridge, noticed. Torstad was not pleased.

"I like my privacy," says Torstad. Torstad, who lives in suburban St. Paul, cannot actually see McCanney's house from his own, but "what seems like a lot of room in the Cities doesn't seem like that much room up here." While he claims no hostility toward McCanney, Torstad wants to preserve his quiet. He worried too, that McCanney's comings and goings would necessitate costly maintenance on the rough track over rock, creek and woods he says cost him $7,000 to build 10 years ago.

Because he didn't want permanent company on his road and until McCanney did the neighborly thing and came around to talk money, Torstad had a gate erected where his road turns off County 71. Torstad doesn't actually own the first 660' (one city block) of his road, but he has what he says is a permanent easement through the property of Richard and Dorothy Knecht, the same kind of easement he's reluctant to grant McCanney.

But if Torstad views the situation through his attitudes on personal space, the Knecht's sentiments are a bit more entrenched. With 165 acres in Moose Valley, the Knecht's are the largest property owners on this section of the ridge and they feel a dimension of stewardship goes along with the title.

The Knecht's don't really want McCanney to complete his chalet and have refused to negotiate his use of the road. "It's not a public road at all, it's a private driveway," says Dorothy Knecht, betraying a dulcet Joan Collins-like accent.

Richard Knecht poses the question in terms of "responsible development." He points out that McCanney's project is only the second in a stretch of 100 miles from Two Harbors to the Canadian Border, which mars the grandeur of the Ridge. "Just imagine the impact of this kind of negative siting," he says in reference to the cabin's bluff setting, "multiplied a hundred times."

The Knechts, who arrived in Moose Valley 11 years ago from Ohio (the other party to the road, the Harrisons, live in Michigan), insist they are not "nasty people" out to rob some other person's vision of happiness. Yet they feel McCanney's chalet is not the kind of "unobtrusive" development that meets all the criteria of compatibility to the existing community in terms of size, shape and color.

Knecht says McCanney's project is "questionable" on a number of grounds excluding the matter of trespass and, like some previous development schemes slated for the valley, deserved to be weeded out by the Cook County zoning committee during the permit process.

That's precisely the point says McCanney, who went to court in 1989 to gain a permanent easement to the road. The county did issue a building permit - admittedly after construction began - based on a minimum lot size of 10 acres. Therefore, says McCanney, he has a legal right to the road because his chalet is "inaccessible" from below except by foot or ATV. (Paul Flood, of the U.S. Forest Service, says McCanney cannot upgrade the path from his acreage below the ridge because of "unacceptable environmental consequences.")

But the Cook County Board and a Grand Marais judge refused to grant McCanney a permanent easement. Cook County attorney, Don Davison, says the cartway easement law from which McCanney sought relief, requires the petitioner to own "5 inaccessible acres." "He (McCanney) failed to prove he owns 5 acres on the ridge."

Davison says that if McCanney were to prove he owns the required lot size, the county would be forced to grant easement. McCanney says he owns more than 5 acres; the holder of a Master's degree in Physics, he surveyed the ridge himself. That's not good enough for Davison who insists McCanney have an official survey of the southwest corner of the section performed.

Everyone involved admits that such a survey would cost many thousand dollars and expose a tangle of inaccurate property descriptions.

Torstad, another person who did his own survey, says the rugged terrain of the ridge and inadequate equipment of early survey teams could mean up to a 15% variation between county records and actual property lines. "It's a problem the whole county has, a lot of property changes hands up here with no one really knowing where the corners are," says Torstad who discovered a neighbors' fence 50' onto his land.

McCanney suggests that the Knechts closed their portion of the road in order to force him to have an official survey done (the other three corners of the section are complete) that they could then use to subdivide their property for development. He notes that a survey could very well prove that the Knecht's have built their home on yet another neighbor's property. He also implies that he ran afoul of the Knechts some years ago when he refused their invitation to join a costly move to electrify the valley.

He says his strong environmental positions may have contributed to his public relations problems in a remote locale where many residents depend on resource extraction. His opposition to the sale of forest service timber on the ridge and his efforts to stop the trapping of rare pine martins in the area may not have been expeditious when trapping interests and the owner of the largest sawmill in northern Minnesota have seats on the County Board.

Like the Knechts and Torstad, he says he wants to live quietly in peace with his neighbors — once he has finished his dream home.

Meanwhile hawks twist on updrafts from the ridge and large fish sit in ambush beneath the waves.

Chapter 5

BWCA

Land of 10,000 Dying Lakes?
SO² Happens

In 1406, the English Parliament ordered death by hanging for anyone caught burning coal within the limits of London. Ever since, we have been increasingly aware of the murderous effects of "bad air."

Authorities have for some time known that the cause of the lethal four-day fog in London, December 1952, which claimed 2,484 lives via bronchitis, coronaries and other lung and heart diseases, was the result of the burning of fossil-fuels.

According to the Council on Environmental Quality (CEQ) "140,000 deaths a year in the U.S. can be attributed, directly or indirectly, to air pollution." Among the 33 most developed countries, life expectancy (1986-87) was shortest among the six Eastern European countries, Yugoslavia, and the Soviet Union. The leading cause of death proved to be cardio-vascular disease and cancer. Air pollution behind the former "Iron Curtain" is virtually unchecked.

Air pollution is such an insidious problem, touching so many aspects of our lives, and our current air standards are so inadequate that we are literally standing on the brink of anni-hilation - paying billions to electric utilities and car manufac-turers - while living in a permanent state of impaired health and environmental degradation.

As Minnesotans, we are fortunate to have the only state law in the nation limiting airborne pollution. We also have more to lose in terms of amenity that almost any other area of the country.

For we are charged with protecting one of the most vaunted resources on the continent, the Boundary Waters

Canoe Area (BWCA). The real Boundary Waters, as distinguished from the gimmicky Dayton's product, is one of the most heavily visited recreational areas in the country, with 225,000 annual guests. It is a unique habitat for a variety of life forms unknown elsewhere in the lower 48.

We're now called upon to witness the destruction of this superb setting. We know why it is dying and we know who is killing it. The facts have been in our hands for many years, as these lakes have moved from "potential harm," the category of disinterest, to "inevitable extinction," the category of alarm.

Although we have arbitrarily assigned ourselves "10,000" lakes, only 4,000 are much larger than Loring Pond. And many of these lakes are prone to irreversible damage due to pollution.

According to a 1981 survey quoting Dave Thornton, Acid Rain Coordinator for the Minnesota Pollution Control Agency (PCA), the latest estimate by that agency following a sampling of 165 lakes from every section of the BWCA, doomed 73% of the areas' 1,493 lakes to virtual sterility in 20 to 40 years at current rates of atmospheric dumping of air pollutants.

Gary Glass, chief researcher for the federal Environmental Protection Agency (EPA) Lab in Duluth, was not an optimist either when it came to Minnesota's chances of avoiding the macabre aquatic wreckage of lake acidification. He figured nearly 250 BWCA lakes in the "very sensitive" index, already experiencing reproductive failure, with complete acidification only 5-10 years away.

Not only is 90% of acid deposition coming from outstate with penalties for non-compliance still a decade off, but our own standard is ten times more corrosive than "normal rain."

Boundary Waters lakes are not the only Minnesota lakes endangered, however. In fact, half the state east of a line between the Twin Cities and International Falls contain lakes at risk.

Out of Stack, Out of Mind

The Industrial Revolution began in England around 1850 and was heavily dependent on the burning of coal and gas to power an immense increase in factory labor. Foul-smelling gases, soot and respiratory illnesses were an indisputable element of urban life in the late 19th and early 20th centuries.

As fossil-fuel combustion increased, local conditions grew intolerable. Eventually, citizen anger threatened anarchy and a novel solution to the problem was found.

Since it was the 'ambient' or immediately surrounding conditions which were suffering disfigurement, higher smoke stacks allowed upper-level winds to disperse the plume of dirty particulate matter downwind. Consequently, the U.S.'s first attempt at air pollution control, the Clean Air Act of 1970, allowed stack heights to be raised to a point where the downwash of pollutants in the immediate vicinity would be nearly invisible.

The following decade became known as the era of the 'superstack' as coal-burning utilities and ore smelters vied to meet the Act's local air standards. While, before 1970, the nation had only two stacks over 500', the U.S. and Canada now have 200 utility stacks 400-1,200 feet in height.

The "super-stacks" did not reduce pollutants (the tallest, International Nickel's (INCO) Sudbury, Ontario stack reaches 1/4 mile high and produces 3% of all sulfur dioxide in North America), but after the style of crisis-management, they did flush the problem downwind. The difficulty of burning fossil fuels, though masked, still existed: coal and petroleum are essentially vegetable matter fossilized over hundreds of millions of years.

As plant matter they contain small amounts of sulfur and nitrogen. Poorly burned in too great a mixture of air, coal and oil combined with oxygen (21% of air) to form oxides of nitrogen and sulfur. Along with ash and other solids (many of them poisonous), these gases are shot up the flue at incredible velocities owning to the rifle barrel effect of enormous stack height.

Sulfur dioxide (SO^2) and nitrogen oxides (NOx) compounds are unstable and undergo significant changes as they mount in the stack's billowing plume. As fine liquid and solid particles, sulfur and nitrogen compounds are known to build up in stagnant high pressure cells one to two miles above ground during hot summer weather.

Plucked by prevailing winds they ride long distances (up to 1,000 miles in five days) in the upper atmosphere. Here they are altered by solar radiation through a complicated, little-understood process known as oxidation. The result, in the case of the sulfur dioxide is sulfate (SO^4) or sulfuric acid (H^2SO^4) raining from the sky. Compounds of sulfate, sulfuric and nitric acids react easily with water, the universal solvent.

The Long Range Transport of Atmospheric Pollutants (LRTAP) was first analyzed and described in 1968 by Swedish scientist Svante Oden while studying the negative effects of acid precipitation on trout reproduction in neighboring Norway.

(Today in Norway, fish population damage has been conclusively proven in an area of 33,000 sq. km. or an area slightly less than half the size of Minnesota. In a third of this area, fish are extinct. Norway's southern coastal area, heavily dependent on European tourism, is predicted to eventually lose 20,000 to 50,000 lakes to acidification.)

Similarly, the pH scale - a measurement of electrical activity within a hydrogen molecule - was developed in Sweden in 1923 as a means of measuring the acidity or alkalinity of aqueous solutions. The pH scale has since become the yardstick of survival and productivity for all aquatic organisms.

The pH scale runs from 1 to 14; values from 1 to 7 indicate the power of hydrogen molecules to turn solutions to acids. Values from 7 to 14 register the ability of base, or alkaline, compounds such as calcium and magnesium to neutralize acids. In the middle or 'neutral' site on the scale is pH 7 — distilled water.

The pH scale is logarithmic, that is - like the famous Richter earthquake scale - an increase of one degree represents a tenfold increase in severity over the previous value. Thus, stomach acid and battery acid (pH 1.5) are ten times more acidic than lemon juice (pH 2.5), 100 times more acidic than table wine (pH 3.5) and a thousand times more acidic than tomato juice (pH 4.5).

"Normal" rain, reflecting a world sullied by sulfur dioxide from volcanoes, forest and cooking fires, is slightly acidic at 5.6 on the pH scale. Unfortunately, rain with a pH under 2 was reported as early as 1978 in the coal-burning valley of Wheeling, W. Virginia.

Too much rock and too little soil put some lakes at risk to acid rain.

Rain with a pH of tomato juice (pH 4.5) was reported to have cut forest growth in Maine by 50% as far back as 1972, and precipitation of pH 4.1 has been common over Massachusetts for the past 20 years.

Rain with a similarly low pH has been detected falling at Hovland on the North Shore of Lake Superior for much of the last decade. In fact, the overall rainfall standard established by the Minnesota Pollution Control Agency (MPCA) for the year 2,000 is 4.7 pH!

Fortunately, most Minnesota lakes can withstand increased inputs of acidic precipitation. Such doses do little harm to the eutrophic, or well-nourished lakes of southern and western Minnesota. (Alas, recent data from the Chesapeake Bay suggests that excessive nitrogen - the nitrogen oxides from power plant emissions and automobile exhaust - can accelerate eutrophication to the point where rapid algal growth chokes off oxygen and sunlight damaging coastal fisheries).

These eutrophic lakes have a high pH index and are amply provided with dissolved calcium carbonate from underlying limestone rock, or from minerals washed into the lake from surrounding soils. Such waters are said to be adequately "buffered" in the same sense that one takes a Rolaids (calcium carbonate) to counteract excess stomach acid.

127

In northeastern and north central portions of Minnesota however, are youthful oligotrophic lakes. Oligotrophic lakes are nutrient poor, lacking the calcium and other minerals which go toward neutralizing acidity thus making for a crowded, happy aquatic environment.

These lakes were formed when the glaciers of 15,000 years ago scraped the topsoil from much of Ontario, Wisconsin and Minnesota and pushed it southward to become the farmland of the Midwest. In the scoured-out granite basins which remained, a multitude of deep, cold lakes were formed by the melting ice sheet.

The soil in this section of the state is very thin, maybe only a couple feet covering bedrock. There is almost no calcereous, or calcium carbonate bearing structure here. This is an area of soft-water lakes with steep, rocky shores. These are the lakes of the Boundary Waters.

Whereas hard-water lakes have dissolved calcium carbonate above 85 ppm (parts per million) and relatively high pH (from 6.8-7.4), the soft-water lakes of the north average less than 40 ppm and their pHs are correspondingly lower, between 5.8-6.6. (200 state lakes have a pH of 5.1). These lakes have neither the productivity of eutrophic lakes (sometimes only a tenth as much) nor the resistance to airborne acidity.

John (Jack) Skrypek, DNR Acid Rain Task Force, outlines the dangerous situation facing the oligotrophic lakes of the BWCA: "In the BWCA alkalinity has historically been in the 10-20 ppm range; now a few lakes are showing less than 5. They are becoming softer and softer. We might soon be seeing borderline effects where lakes are starting to change."

Acid Pulses

Twin Cities eutrophic lakes have safe alkalinities in the range of 150 ppm. But if, as in the BWCA, calcium is a mere trace element, disaster is just around the corner.

As the last particles of calcium react with incoming acids and fall out of solution, pH will drop--not slowly over a period of decades, but explosively. In a flash of geologic time simple water molecules will be converted into an increasingly powerful acid solution. Soon the magic pH of 6 is reached — beyond this point lakes face inexorable damage.

Even before the lake itself becomes 10 times (a drop from 7 to 6 pH) more acidic than distilled water, young fish and the insect populations upon which they feed, may disappear. The culprit is a build-up of acidic precipitation in snow during the winter and the sudden flush of this concentrated acid into the lake in early spring.

Spring thaws can thus create temporary, but fatal, drops in pH levels, turning the thin layer of surface water in which walleye eggs and larvae hatch into a crematorium where the tiny fry are cooked in a bath of sulfuric acid 100 times more reactive than their normal environment.

Whole classes of young fish can be wiped out in this way, prior to visible damage to adult fish. The lake may appear healthy when it has in fact already lost an entire year's population. At or near the level where walleye embryos are killed by springtime acid pulses, female smallmouth bass may experience reproductive failure.

The Canadian government has documented the fadeout during the 1950's of smallmouth from a string of lakes in the La Cloche Mountains near Sudbury, Ontario. (The nearby INCO ore smelter annually emits more sulfur dioxide than all the world's volcanoes.)

Walleyes were next to go, in the mid-60's, as pH dipped below 6; lake trout ceased reproduction at 5.5. Walleyes and trout are extremely sensitive and their disappearance was noted even while prey species were still abundant. The vestiges of a once-healthy fish community was, in La Cloche, finally reduced to a population of white suckers, many of them with spinal deformities from the acid which ate at their spinal calcium.

Evidence from Canada's Experimental Lakes Area project and elsewhere suggest it is not only fish, but nearly every living organism in the lake which faces extinction. As lake pH dips toward 5.5, frogs, crawfish, snails, insects and salamanders fail to reproduce. Leaf litter, normally a source of calcium in a healthy lake, fails to decompose as microbes and bacteria die off.

Organic debris accumulate in the bottom of the lake and nutrient recycling slows. Plant and animal plankton suffer and less energy is transferred to higher links in the food chain.

Although the lake is dying at pH 5, large fish may still remain, though their numbers will be fewer. Small fish will not be in evidence. The lake pH may even pause here temporarily, its descent halted by the replacement of calcium by magnesium and other trace buffering minerals.

But it's at this point that the cruelest twist of acid fate is discovered. Although the sheer stress of plunging pH is sufficient to inhibit the reproduction of most aquatic creatures, the final killer of the lake, the finishing *coup de grace* which will render the waters uninhabitable for eternity (it is now too late for expensive remedial liming) is the mobilization of poisonous heavy metals from bottom sediments.

Heavy metals such as mercury, cadmium and aluminum are present throughout the environment but are normally held out of the water column by alkaline compounds. When these compounds are themselves tied up in reaction to the hydrogen ions in sulfuric acid, the heavy metals are free to interact directly with aquatic life with dire consequences.

Since 1979, the Minnesota Department of Health has maintained a health alert for mercury in eleven lakes on the edge of the BWCA, including White Iron, Burntside, Crane, Basswood, Trout, Gunflint and the east arm of Rainy Lake. Fish from these lakes have shown elevated levels of mercury in muscle tissue which may be dangerous for the fetuses of pregnant women, young children and those who eat more than ten fish meals per month.

John Matta of the Health Dept.'s Environmental Health section says pike from Basswood have averaged .42 ppm of mercury and walley .61 ppm in sample fillets. For humans, such concentrations in the bloodstream would be twice to three times the amount suspected of creating impairment of vision and brain function, and over 20 times that capable of producing birth defects. (The Federal Food and Drug Administration will not allow fish with a concentration of .5 ppm to be imported into the U.S.).

Matta underlines the need for care in comparing mercury levels in fish tissue to mercury levels in the bloodstream of humans who consume them. "I wouldn't say the average sportfisherman is in any danger; you would have to be a rather steady consumer, over two meals a week for long periods of time. But I would be concerned for some of the people who live up there, especially if they eat a lot of big fish."

Perhaps the most sinister toxic metal brought to life by sulfuric acid is aluminum. Acidified waters always demonstrate an unusually high concentation of aluminum ions. Above a pH of 5, aluminum is not soluble; at pH 4.3, aluminum kills fish in four days.

As acidification continues, certain acid-loving mosses and a few fungi creep into the lake environment now deserted by oxygen-dependent species. The waters clarify — there are no minerals in suspension.

The lake can still be canoed, and will cool a swimmer. But there are no insects, no fish and no birds. There are no lilies for moose to feed upon, no snails or frogs for raccoons. At pH 4.5 the lake is no longer a part of the wild; it is as cold and lifeless as the moon.

How Widespread a Problem is Acid Rain?

Acid rain over the U.S. is about 70% sulfur dioxide and 30% nitrogen (mostly from auto fuels). Electric power generation produces half of the approximately 26 million tons of sulfur dioxide released annually by U.S. industry; Canadian sources contribute about 7 million tons of airborne pollutants.

Thanks to the colossal super-stacks, it's hardly a local problem, with a reputed 75-90% of the acid rain falling over Minnesota generated elsewhere. About 90% of sulfur dioxide and 60% of nitrogen oxides originate in the "acid corridor": the Ohio River Valley with its 10 mammoth high-sulfur coal-fired utility plants in a 250-mile line from Portsmith, Ohio to Louisville, Kentucky, is responsible for one-quarter of U.S. emissions.

(Recent atmospheric modelling, however, suggests Texas, the country's largest NO^2 emitter - 6th largest SO^2 transporter - is the chief source of SO^2 deposition in Minnesota.)

Vulnerable locations - those with thin, unbuffered soils - stand to lose the most. The Adirondack Mountains for instance, one of the most beautiful of the acid-sensitive regions east of the Mississippi, has been severely impacted in the last 50 years.

131

More than 250 lakes in the Adirondacks at elevations above 2,000 feet, including Lake Colden, once the most highly prized trout fishing in the east, and Lake Tear of the Clouds, the source of the Hudson River, are now acidic. Efforts to revive Lake Colden with liming (calcium oxide) and restocking of fish populations failed due to accumulation of toxic aluminum ions. The EPA judges 60% of all Northeast lakes to be at risk with little capacity to neutralize more acid.

Hundreds of lakes in Quebec are showing acid stress and in Nova Scotia, 20 rivers once thick with salmon have seen steep declines in pH since 1960. In neighboring Ontario, the figures are ghoulish: Toronto officials expect to lose 50,000 lakes (the Province has 250,000) at today's rate of sulfate loadings. Unfortunately, all these areas are similar in geology, climate and fish species composition to our own BWCA.

In Europe, acid rain was ignored before the following dismal tally came in: 9.1 million acres or half of W. Germany's forests - including the famous Black Forest - are dying. Evergreens and firs are the first to suffer premature loss of needles leaving trees weakened and prey to wind, drought and disease.

Switzerland claims a third of its forests are dying and with their death, huge landslides are occuring in mountain valleys where trees no longer anchor the soil.

East European countries Hungry, Poland, East Germany, Czechoslovakia and Romania face major environmental crisis due to acid rain; lakes in Georgia have experienced mutations; and "rapid deterioration" of southern commercial forests has been noted.

Alpine lakes in the Rocky Mountains and Sierra Nevadas report damage from coal-fired utilities and smelters in northern New Mexico, Arizona and Mexico; some Colorada lakes report reproductive failure in salamanders.

Can Anything Be Done?

Minnesota utilities now produce 110,000 tons of sulfur dioxide annually. From 20-30% of this amount finds its way northward to the three million acre Quetico-Superior wildernesses of Minnesota and Ontario. Canadian sources - including 77,000 tons of SO^2 emitted annually from the 400 megawatt

Atikokan plan 100 miles from the BWCA - account for about 30% of the sulfur and nitrogen pollution which threatens the region.

This is not to say that all is lost, however. Fully 50% of nitrogen oxides could be eliminated simply by a more efficient mixture of air and fuel during combustion. Such technology, including Flue Gas Desulfurization (bathing flue gases in a neutralizing solution of calcium carbonate), is occasionally mandated on new power plants.

Yet existing stacks are unregulated with no retrofitting required. And due to a levelling off of energy demand, fewer new plants are coming on line to replace old, dirty facilities. Also, with diminishing stocks of world oil, pressure will mount to relax emission standards on the use of high-sulfur coal. Already a de-regulatory political climate and economic recession have stymied efforts to put tighter restrictions on auto emissions.

Canada, as befitting its role as steward of the giant's share of North America's fresh water resources, has done the most of any nation to cleanse its skies of acid rain. The Canadian government has vowed to cut SO^2 emissions 50% by 1994. Even the giant INCO smelter at Sudbury has agreed to cut its emissions by 2/3.

Canada, of course, has to make reductions not only to put its own house in order, but also to have some leverage over the United States which is responsible for half the poisoning taking place in the Canadian atmosphere. Nor can Canadians neglect good relations with neighboring Minnesota which receives an estimated 10-15% of its acidic deposition from Canada (2% from Ontario).

Europe has responded as well, though belatedly and on a lesser scale. In 1983, 14 nations including Great Britain, W. Germany, and the Soviet Union, signed an agreement to reduce acidic emissions 30% by 1994. The U.S. refused to become a signatory.

The U.S. during the Reagan years, could not bring itself to regard the situation as critical. While some of this reluctance was based on a perceived need for long-range data and more accurate atmospheric modelling, much of it was simple politics. The Reagan administration wanted to present an image of holding the line on taxes, and a $5-15 billion national program (estimated) - even if only $1.40 more on the monthly utility bill

133

- would have tarnished that image. (The $500 billion Savings & Loan bail-out did not have to be faced until Reagan left office.)

Likewise, Reagan voting strength was anchored in the West and acid rain was perceived as an *eastern* problem. Also, the two most likely routes by which utilities could achieve reductions in SO^2 - closing older, inefficient plants or converting from high-sulfur Appalachian coal (3-5%) to low-sulfur western coal (.5%) - would have cost 38,000 jobs and alienated union support. (Other paths to cleaner air - installing expensive stack scrubbers, increased dependence on nuclear power or encouraging energy conservation - were viewed as encumbered with political negatives.)

The picture has changed thanks to the 1990 revisions of the Clean Air Act. According to Rick Strassman of the Minnesota Pollution Control Agency's air quality division, a national reduction in SO^2 of 50% is scheduled by the year 2,000.

Lowered emissions are not a sure-fire thing, however, owing to the market-driven nature of the revised Act. While the 1995 target date for cleaning up the U.S.'s 111 dirtiest coal-fired plants looks good on paper, the process is, not surprisingly, a bit cloudy. Utility companies will be given a number of options - scrubbers, low-sulfur coal, shut-down or purchase "allowances" - in order that they may find their own path to compliance.

In the case of 'allowances,' a dirty plant may continue to pollute - even increase its SO^2 emissions - if its operation remains sufficiently profitable to buy the 'allowances' that the EPA plans to grant utility systems already meeting national standards. In other words, thanks to NSP forsight - and rate-payer forebearance - the Minnesota utility will be able to sell an 'allowance' (a ton of SO^2) to dirty outstate polluters who find it too onerous to clean-up themselves.

That's because Minnesota struck at acid rain early. In 1982, the Minnesota legislature passed the Acid Deposition Control Act which required: a) designation of sensitive areas; b) a control plan for reducing emissions beyond existing levels; and c) penalties to force compliance by 1990. Today the state produces less SO^2 than it did in 1980 and substantially less than allowed by the MPCA to protect the environment.

This means that local utilities have clean air 'allowances', or tons of SO^2 deficits, they can trade on the commodities market like so much grain. While NSP is not shy in trumpeting its early role in emissions reduction, it remains to be seen whether 'allowances' sold by the company will go to repay the $300 million borrowed from rate-payers for clean-up equipment, or will wind up in shareholders pockets as "profit".

Then too, it's not clear what kind of "standards" the Environmental Protection Agency (EPA) will adopt for the nation's utility systems. Environmentalists recall that while the out-going Carter administration tried to enact tougher U.S. standards to protect Canada in 1981, it was the Reagan appointed EPA staff that successfully blocked the effort grounds that "danger" was more concept than empirical fact. Nor did the Reagan EPA review and revise SO_2 standards every five years as required by the Clean Air Act. (Minnesota and several other states went to court to force the EPA to carry out this mandate.)

The revised 1990 Act depends on EPA enforcement and still allows plenty of hot, polluted air to circulate as creation of technical standards, risk assessments and granting of automatic extensions could potentially delay clean-up for as much as 20 years beyond the target dates. Still, Minnesota at least, has been given a breathing spell in terms of acid deposition.

The two dirtiest Minnesota plants - the Allen S. King plant (NSP) in Stillwater and the Clay Boswell plant (Minnesota Power) near Grand Rapids - have had emissions cut 50% and 20% respectively. All in-state point sources must have an operating permit quantifying emissions. And preliminary reports indicate that Minnesota has cut its stack emissions in half since 1980. But are the state's sensitive areas safe?

On the surface, man-made safeguards fall short: the statewide rainfall standard is 4.7 pH - 10 times more acidic than normal rain - is still exceeded in some areas and would be if every source in Minnesota were shut down. The fact is, 90% of atmospheric SO_2 falling in the state comes from outside the state.

Yet an unexpected accident of geography has positioned Minnesota on the "safe edge" of acid precipitation, says David Thornton. Newer lake data and more sophisticated atmospheric modelling leads to the conclusion that no Boundary Waters lakes have been acidified — nor are they likely to be.

Thornton says that Minnesota has been lucky; the BWCA lakes in the 'sensitive' category of the early 1980's - the 5-20 ppm alkalinity lakes - are safe, claims Thornton. Only heavier

135

doses of acidity would place them at risk and, "in general, acid rain appears to be lessening thanks to the Clean Air Act."

The "truly sensitive" lakes are those with 0-5 ppm alkalinity. They are small lakes perched above the water table with no streams entering or leaving their basin. Minnesota has such lakes, a couple hundred estimates Thornton, but they are not in the northeast where they might be suseptible to long-range atmospheric transport from the Ohio River Valley.

Instead, Minnesota's perched lakes with low alkalinity are in the north central/north west area of the state near Fergus Falls. Ironically, such lakes in Minnesota are not in danger because of 'pollution' from North and South Dakota in the form of alkaline dust which neutralizes acid inputs.

Lakes of similar composition located in north central Wisconsin have been acidified says Thornton because they lack alkaline dust to neutralize the greater level of acid deposition they receive from the industrialized east.

"Ten years ago we were concerned," Thornton summarizes, "but the new Clean Air Act should lead to a detectable lessening in airborne acidity and a larger safety margin for Minnesota lakes."

We should take some comfort in this news. This is, after all, a victory for the environment that every outdoor enthusiast can celebrate — for a moment. Then it's time to gear up for battle against the 2.7 billion tons of industrial toxins released annually into the U.S. environment which aren't regulated. Or, begin notifying our representatives with concerns about airborne PCB's and dioxion over the Great Lakes. Or take on the darling of the 90's, the claim that another gas, carbon dioxide, will create a greenhouse effect dooming the BWCA to become a palm tree desert surrounded by cotton farms.

Underwater Treasure

The BWCA hiker is surrounded by a rich trove of scenic delights, from gem-green pines to blue and white skies softer than the belly plumage on a whiskey jack. The canoeist slides serenely along atop a magical chemistry of cobalt hues listening to the deep sounds of the planet's beginning. Those who fish savor the presence of large predators — a heart-pounding eruption of water at the end of a thin, naked filament.

But what of that other realm beneath the azure heavens, beside the emerald trees and beyond the zone of free-swimming fishes? What of the bottom of this watery wilderness? Do we not save a thought for this exotic, albeit sodden, environment?

I am referring of course to the bottom of the 1,800 Boundary Waters lakes. Here treasure awaits in forms both various and valuable. To visit this world, simply don a swimsuit and slip below the waves. Keep your eyes focused on the shadowy lake floor with its sharply angled nooks and dark unexplored crannies.

Ignore if you can the crescent-shaped claws of the crayfish, beware the iron jaws of the ancient snapping turtle, smirk if you must at the comical frog, but remember your mission: sunken treasure. For as pristine as this wilderness is, with skies swept clean by powerful drafts and signs of terrestrial habitation expunged by diligent forestry workers, there still exists hidden evidence of human cultures which have left their mark under the dancing waters.

Not that all of these goodies arrived in the abyss willingly. Many were plucked from unwary visitors by Neptune and his aroused minions. But if you are up for a challenge descend with me into the depths and see for yourself the vault and its lode.

Among the 'jewels' I have unearthed (!) are a Medalist fly-reel (complete with fly-line, backing and tippet), a Chicago cutlery filet knife (and sheath), an antique oil lamp, a couple of anchors, a cooler, yes, even some golf balls, and several hundred lures some of which proved to be rare and valuable.

Diving in the BWCA need not be sophisticated, costly or cumbersome. You are not required to use a wet-suit and weight-belt and scuba (Jacques Cousteau's celebrated Self-Contained Underwater Breathing Apparatus) tanks. Naturally, such equipment will lengthen your stay underwater and provide a degree of comfort in these chilly granitic basins. But renting such equipment is expensive, transport is a burden and operating it forces one to develop a level of skill both costly and time-consuming.

The unaided diver does want a decent (watertight) mask ($25) and swim fins ($30). Oddly enough, I found my mask corrected myopia, but I'd use it anyway to avoid bloodshot eyeballs. A neoprene skin diving helmet is also a good idea to protect against rapid heat loss (most body heat is lost through the head). Swim fins stir up bottom silt and thus obscure visibility so try to keep them well beyond your current area of interest. They are very useful not only for quick lateral travel but also for getting to the surface promptly for a breath of air.

Confine your diving to the littoral area of the lake, or that area along the shore to a depth of 15'. Not only is this the area of greatest potential discovery, but it also receives sufficient light to make finds possible. And of course, diving without scuba to depths greater than 15' can result in severe (and painful) pressure in the sinus cavities. You will no doubt observe the thermocline at a depth of 8'-10' during early summer when warm surface water gives way to colder 40 degree chill.

To find sunken lures you need only follow the many strands of monofilament line which stretch across the bottom some 20-30' off of most popular campsites. But do be careful. Those artificials are there for a reason: they have a great many hooks that became snagged on the craggy rocks below. In all likelihood they are still snagged so follow that line cautiously. Mono takes a very long time to degrade and it's probably strong

Davy Jones Locker looted by treasure seekers.

enough to trap you underwater should you foolishly wrap it around your hand or leg!

Either carry a small blade with you to cut the mono if you do become entangled or attack only one line per dive. In the latter case, you can collect the mono slowly, rising to the surface for breath periodically until you locate precisely the rock which has caught someone's terminal tackle. Then, fill up your lungs, execute a perfect surface dive (remember to kick the feet up

139

high for proper vertical entry), and get to the bottom in just a few seconds.

The lure is no doubt trapped beneath a rock too large to move so don't even try. Simply find the leader on one side of the rock and, using your other hand, reach to the opposite side and pull outward (toward deep water). Try to find the hooks first. They may be rusted and ready to break (hooks usually oxidize in a relatively short time) but you still don't want to put one in your finger.

Also, your treasure looks better in its original condition whatever it might be. So try to recover the entire artifact instead of breaking off the old hooks and replacing them with shiny new ones. Unless, of course, your find is so ordinary you plan on casting (and losing?) it again. Otherwise, retire it to a display case. It's done it's job and you can get more out of it as a conversation piece anyway.

Please remove as much monofilament as you safely can. Not only does it not belong, but it can be a hazard to turtles, diving birds and even creatures as large and agile as otters.

Part of the excitement of diving for treasure in the BWCA is the possibility of uncovering unique tackle, the do-it-yourself weaponry of the old-timers, who sought their quarry before the era of plastic extrusion and mass merchandising.

In fact, several pieces in my collection have so far defied analysis by the 'experts'. Well, not exactly. We may know it's a sinker but we don't know how it was used, or in the case of one lure made of iron with (yes, it's true) 15 hooks, we can only guess it's intended victim was a coelacanth.

Here are a few pointers to keep in mind when selecting your treasure lake: Go for a rocky bottom; sandy bottom lakes such as North and South Fowl just can't grab and hold those lures for you. Pick clean water. Of course, all BWCA lakes are clean but tea-stained waters don't offer the water clarity - especially at depths of 10' or more where you will be operating - diving demands. Be careful not to choose a lake that's deep because deep lakes (over 60'-80') are often very cold lakes as well.

Popular lakes quite naturally have more campsites and thus more diving opportunities. But lakes off the regular touristy routes just may yield some rather unique oddities and they are less likely to have been picked over on prior dives.

Remember to dive with a companion for safety's sake and if you happen to find a large silver rapala you can return it to me care of the publisher.

What of the Wolf —
Thriving or Surviving?

Minnesota still has wilderness thank God, though we no longer have an abundance of it and some forms are gone forever. As a dominant predator which has resisted consistent efforts to exterminate it, the wolf is the symbol of Minnesota's commitment to preserving environmental conditions favorable to both wild and non-wild alike.

That the wolf is with us yet is by no means based on a solid consensus for the wolf remains an enigma. All manner of belief circulates as to its powers, its range, even its appearance.

In northern Minnesota, the wolf is regarded as something of a varmit and approximately 300 wolves annually are illegally trapped, poisoned or shot. The federal government, with official power over the wolf, considers it a "threatened" species in this state allowing a legal harvest of 80 wolves a year. And the state DNR wants the authority to legalize a portion of the unlawful killing (160 animals) in the belief that a limited program of "predator control" will placate northerner's hostility toward the animal.

What is known about the wolf tells us that it's a very intelligent animal with a highly-specialized group structure that includes birth control, a rigid dominance hierarchy, individual nurturing and a kind of crude social justice. It will also kill and eat anything it can get its paws on.

Estimates of its current range and number vary, though Bill Berg, DNR wildlife biologist specializing in large predators, thinks there are "1,200-1,500" in Minnesota. Wolf numbers in the BWCA are "fairly stable." There, climax growth conifer forests have reduce the size of deer herds, the wolves' basic food group.

Berg, who takes wolf census out of his Grand Rapids office, says wolf populations are expanding outside the Superior National Forest ranging over the northern half of the state all the way to Little Falls and Lake Mille Lacs south of Pine City. Berg points out that extensive cultivation of aspen provides young trees - brose - for deer inevitably increasing resources to wolves.

But their numbers have not actually increased, says Berg, because of the volume of legal and illegal killing. And there's even an 'Accidental Death' category to the wolf-man interface: several dozen annually depart the woods after encountering Uniroyals and Bridgestones. "It's a fact, wolves commonly end up under tires," according to Berg.

False wolf sightings have mushroomed of late, owing their dubious origins to the fact that the wolf is only a single member, albeit a large and undomesticated one, of the dog family. Physiologically, it's almost impossible to tell the difference between a wolf, a coyote or any other members of the canine contingent, according to Berg.

Coyotes are often mistaken for wolves, says Carroll Henderson, head of the DNR's Non-game Wildlife Program, as are coyote-dog hybrids. Coyote-wolf hybrids and dog-wolf crosses seldom occur since wolves generally eat rather than mate coyotes and domestic dogs.

Confusion also results from the fact that coyotes are widespread and of varying size. An adult Minnesota coyote (sometimes euphemistically referred to as a "brush wolf") of 40- 45 lbs. is smaller than the Maine type (crossed with the Algonquin wolf of Ontario) but larger than that of the South-west, producing an offspring nearly as big as the yearling eastern timber wolf found here.

Similarly, were a coyote to breed with a dog as large as the wolf such as a German shepherd or a malamute, it could produce adult offspring in the typical wolf range of 60-90 lbs. Large wolves, in the 110-120 lb. vicinity, are not common.

Coyotes are far more ubiquitous than wolves, ranging border to border with a breeding population of 20,000-25,000 says the DNR. That figure is doubled after breeding but annual mortality among coyotes may be 25% or higher. Coyotes, of course, are not protected and can be taken in season by trapping or hunting; about 15,000 coyotes are eradicated annually by these means.

The accuracy of any visual sighting probably depends on where the animal was and what it was doing, maintain Henderson and Jim Engle, Endangered Species Co-ordinator for the U.S. Forest Service, North Central Region. Engle claims that enzyme analysis obtained from the animal's carcass or skull will lead to "overwhelming proof" of its true lineage but says such forensic efforts are seldom required.

"The difficulty arising from coyote-dog hybrids - and the grey area caused by accidental shootings, 'I thought it was a coyote,' - make prosecution under the Endangered Species Act unlikely," Engle explains.

But they do occur, says Dave Duncan, Special Aide with the U.S. Fish and Wildlife Service, Duluth. Duncan investigates "20- 30" wolf killings a year with about 10% resulting in prosecution. Duncan says that illegally killing a wolf is a misdemeanor crime involving a possible prison sentence and a fine of up to $250,000.

These maximum penalties are generally not invoked, however, because the wolf is "doing well" in Minnesota, says Duncan. As an "endangered" species whose numbers were declining, the wolf would be eligible for maximum protection. But as of 1974, the wolf was reclassified at state request in order to allow for trapping and killing the creature when it is accused

144

of attacking livestock. "Most fines for illegally taking wolves are less than $1,000," says Duncan.

A state fund set up to compensate farmers for wolf depredations paid out $28,000 to cover 49 claims in 1988, according to Ed Bogges, DNR furbearer specialist. These verified wolf kills included two cows, 28 calves, 58 sheep, a pet goat, a duck and 257 turkeys.

Wolves and coyotes share a similar fondness for domestic fare but because of their larger size, wolves have more of a tendency to kill cattle while coyotes lean toward fowl, says Bogges.

Randy Evans, DNR Enforcement officer who oversees the initial investigation in cases of suspected wolf attacks on livestock, believes much of the damage attributed to wolves actually turns out to be coyotes or domestic dogs running wild. He cites the case of 102 turkeys killed in a single evening on a northern farm.

The farmer suspected wolves but evidence turned up by the DNR provided a different picture: "It proved to be a female coyote teaching her pups - they'll have six to eight of them in a single litter - how to kill. Obviously, that many turkeys weren't being killed for food; the pups were learning a lesson and they seemed to enjoy it."

Wolves normally feed on whitetail deer with an adult wolf eating perhaps 15-20 deer in a year. Given the number of wolves in the state that is 20,000 deer. To put the matter in perspective: over 15,000 whitetails are killed annually on state roads, another 75,000 are taken illegally by poachers, 8,000 were taken by bow and arrow and 139,000 (1988) killed during the state's firearm season. Total numbers of deer are increasing and with them the chance that future generations will experience the true meaning of wilderness epitomized in the wolf.

The Ones That Got Away

The Boundary Waters Canoe Area of northern Minnesota is an amphibious fantasyland of 2,000 portage-connected lakes perched like a crown among the fur-trimmed hills of a National Forest so wild it serves as a hotel for wolves.

Over half of the million-acre wilderness is water. These ancient basins are cold and dark, painted the color of diamonds at midnight by thin acidic soils. Some still bear melodious names, whispers of the Ojibway Indian language: mammoth Saganaga translates "lake surrounded by forests;" shallow Kawishiwi is "lake full of beaver lodges;" and Ogishkemuncie, the "kingfisher lake." Captured in a vast net of boreal forest known as the Big Woods, the BWCA is an isolated world linked by high pearly skies and narrow canoe trails - rugged up-hill climbs sometimes a mile or more in length.

The camper must remember that this Camelot blended of water and woodland is nature writ on a celestial scale, a kingdom of the strong where blood is shed relentlessly and beauty masks an indifference to pain. The likelihood of confrontation with the cosmos is so great here, selection of a crew is as necessary as the knowledge of what is poisonous and what merely carnivorous.

Those participating in such an expedition must be hardy souls capable of toting heavy packs by the hour, paddling atop dangerous swells and remembering to dry-pack their toilet paper. It is important therefore, to weed out those who prefer naugahyde and neon over fang and claw.

Through the years we have banded into an eclectic group which accepts the stern ecology of the wild setting; in turn, we allow any number of human eccentricities.

We have a fisherman in Tom. Tom's piscine pursuits suggest the cynic's definition of an angler as 'a fool waiting for a jerk.' A Lindner Bros. groupie, he has collected a vast array of brilliantly-hued weapons crammed into one gigantic tackle box (per species, that is). To judge by results, some varieties Tom chases are extinct. We estimate his next catch at $587 a lb. Tom's saving grace is the sense of humor he retains faced with a majority who believe the only thing worse than fishing, is catching one.

Jacqui's capacity to spend endless hours on a rock communing with the heavens was awesome, particularly during K.P. Her incessant comparison - humanity vs. infinity - led to a ban on all conversations beginning with 'Can you believe how small we are?' Still, we enjoy a campfire philosopher with the spunk to take a moral stand: "Why I would no sooner wish nuclear destruction on the Russians than I'd annihilate South Dakota — and I've lived in South Dakota!"

Unfortunately, not all who camped with us developed a fondness for weekend regression. There was Eddy for instance. Eddy found our annual excursion to the realm of the oversoul too stimulating: we found Eddy too dangerous. He seemed to get lost - not a lot but certainly enough. Eventually we came to understand that his problems were of psychic origins, a product of his refusal to take maps literally.

"You've got to generalize, gen-er-al-ize!" the former geography student lectured as we paddled toward Height of Land Portage. At this magical spot 300 years ago, authentic Voyageurs initiated novices into the fraternity with a quaint ceremony involving cedar boughs, musket fire and an alcoholic beverage related to charcoal starter. I was having trouble finding the put-in; maybe it was the fragrance of alder pollen, or the florescent glow of sprouting leaves — I let Eddy navigate.

Soon Eddy 'generalized' us into abandoning our craft in a licorice-like slough of black mud. Stepping from the canoe, we were confronted by a sullen army of willow saplings. I endured 10 minutes of torture at the hands of these Darwinian zealots before I broke down in tears. Eddy refused to change course, in fact, he refused to answer. Come to think of it, I hadn't seen Eddy since entering this bush-covered rivulet, but

Eddy must be up ahead I reasoned, what else could be making all that noise?

I pushed the canoe forward over a slippery, splintered deadfall and followed, sliding into a tiny slurp of a pond encircled by poplar trees. Suddenly, the waters in front of me grew to a boil. I shuddered and stumbled, staring in wonder as a huge antlered head covered with thick dark hair emerged from the swamp. It looked and smelled like a doormat. I was transfixed; brackish water streamed off the 8-foot withers and tidal waves sucked at its knees.

The animal's eyes were as deep and brown as dirt. We studied each other, the only movement in the universe the serene munching of jaws the size of a Toyota. A moose — and a very real, up-close one at that. I'd seen museum moose but they were not in this guy's league. Despite its enormous bulk, it was not at all grotesque. Indeed, it possessed a chiseled beauty, an ineffable spiritual presence humans can only grope for. The moose chewed; I suspended.

A shaft of sunlight shot through the clouds stirring the pond into slate-black ripples; golden aspen blades spun and chattered in the breeze. The bow of the canoe caught a draft and swung toward the massive ruminant. Slowly, regally, the beast rose above me. "Whoa, whooaaa," I whistled, turning into profile so it might more easily weigh my insignificance. Then, with a slight hydraulic movement of its immense shoulders, it fled. The encounter was brief but unforgettable. I think I'll forgive Eddy — when they find him.

Denise was another case of agoraphobia among the urban elite that ought to occasion an inquiry into the state of public education. Denise's notion of adventure was a trip to Sak's where her will power did battle with a $350 cocktail dress. Proud to be on her first wilderness trek, Denise showed off her gear: lizzard-skin boots, boom box, two oranges and a can of sardines, "I'm dieting."

Denise was a fabulous storyteller; her 'true tales' of the "psychos" she had gone out with kept us next to the fire until we tipped over. But at other times, her intuition let her down. One afternoon I encountered Denise drinking from a small stream. "What do you think?" she asked. "There's nothing chocolaty about this water to me..."

"Hunh?"

148

"Well, Jeff said this water tastes like giardellia. Isn't that a kind of Italian chocolate or something?"

"Wow, Denise, I think he meant the water 'tested' for giardia, it's an intestinal parasite..."

Now on the subject of bugs, I've come by quite a store of information: black flies chain-saw into exposed flesh with a series of razor-edged teeth — not a silly sucking tube mind you, but real ivory. Wood ticks creep about the human body on eight stealthy legs and can only be discovered through intimate inspection. A female mosquito in search of blood may fly 10 miles in a single evening and can drill through Levi 501s. Even the common housefly takes on a malevolent aspect north of Duluth.

I know all this because Larry told me. Larry mumbled such data constantly. He had to.

Larry exuded CO^2 the way school girls give off aura of Ambush. Larry, unfortunately, could not afford the attentions of insects programmed to regard such a scent as occasion for propagating passion. Larry had the habit of swelling. After a couple of bites his face resembled a Gene Fullmer title defense as seen through an aquarium.

With sane investments in the latest bonnets and repellents, Larry managed to keep the BWCA's armed invertebrates at bay until one indescribable bashing. Crossing a windy arm of Basswood Lake at sundown, Larry's canoe tipped and he was forced ashore in the woods some distance from our campsite. It was a hot thick night on an itchy mossy slope in shorts and t-shirt.

Larry was found the next afternoon, eyes swollen shut and mind pumped into delirium by insect toxins, running naked along Hiway 169, eating berries and rushing at cars.

Larry works on a secret military project now and no longer camps. Says it isn't worth it to fortify oneself with repellent or netting, "I've had it with defensive measures!"

Finally, there was Mat. Mat had the reflexes of a mantis on the frame of a hang-glider. Resembling an early Winnebago RV, Mat symbolized the triumph of raw power over design. Blessed with incredible strength and endurance, he was known to inflict pain on inanimate objects.

He also possessed certain disquieting enthusiasms and, although it's highly useful to have one of the party capable of portaging two canoes, one under each arm, we grew wary of Mat's discipline factor. Spying the purple silhouette of an approaching squall, his humanity would suffer a curious disappearance. The dim words of some heavy metal group on his lips, Mat would steer into the fist of the storm. At this point his passengers were introduced to new precincts of psychedelic terror as the deep s'lush, s'lush of his giant stroke mixed with the roll of thunder, whistling 40 mph gusts and the rattle of apple-sized hail. But Mat too, had his limits.

Impatient as always in his quest for Big Water vistas, Mat once scrambled onto an island in order to gain a better view(or to push it out of his way, we weren't sure). As he plunged into the undergrowth, Tom and I knelt to examine a pile of what looked to be the bones of several small animals....

"Hey, hey you! Get back, hey!"

It was Mat's voice alright, but it sounded strained, as if he'd met a problem that couldn't be fixed by applying a little more torque.

"Mat? Mat, where are you?" Tom ventured.

"I'm over here — in a tree!" Mat screamed.

"What happened?" cried Tom.

"Some crazy bear just took a chunk outta my butt!"

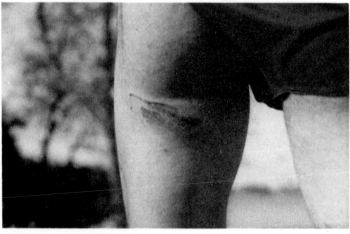

Bears have an uncommon way of giving directions: no bluff here.

Tom and I went over the injury scene; we found a sunfish-colored bruise the size of a ping-pong paddle but the bruin's 4" canines barely broke the skin.

"Bite?" Tom joked, "Hell, it's just a nip. That bear was simply telling you to stay out of her territory, one brute to another."

We tried to convince him that it could have been a whole lot worse but Mat shook us off refusing to recognize any good intentions on the bear's part. To this day he's sore about the incident. His eyes recede under one of the world's more ample brow ridges as he recalls the event, his fingers clenching like a steam bucket, "You know, I thought I was going to have to kill that thing!"

Mat doesn't camp much anymore but he retains his ties to the primitive — he sells bonds.